![DK SMITHSONIAN logo] DK SMITHSONIAN

Did You Know?

amazing answers to the questions you ask

**LONDON, NEW YORK,
MELBOURNE, MUNICH, and DELHI**

Senior Editor Fleur Star
Editorial team Caroline Bingham, Annabel Blackledge, Rod Green,
Rob Houston, Ashwin Khurana, Susan Reuben, Jane Yorke
US Editor Margaret Parrish
Senior Art Editor Spencer Holbrook
Design team Dave Ball, Steve Crozier, Carol Davis, Paul Drislane,
Rachael Grady, Samantha Richiardi, Steve Woosnam-Savage
Illustrators Adam Benton, Peter Bull,
Stuart Jackson-Carter, Arran Lewis
Photoshop Retouching Steve Crozier
Cartography Simon Mumford
Consultants Dr. Jacqueline Mitton (Space), Douglas Palmer (Earth),
Dr. Kim Dennis-Bryan (Living World), Philip Parker (History),
Ian Graham (Science), Dr. Penny Preston (Human Body)

Jacket Editor Maud Whatley
Jacket Designer Laura Brim
Jacket Design Development Manager Sophia MTT
Picture Research Sumedha Chopra
Producer, Pre-production Francesca Wardell
Senior producer Mandy Inness

Managing Editor Gareth Jones
Managing Art Editor Philip Letsu
Publisher Andrew Macintyre
Publishing Director Jonathan Metcalf
Associate Publishing Director Liz Wheeler
Art Director Phil Ormerod

Smithsonian

This trademark is owned by the Smithsonian Institution and
is registered in The United States Patent and Trademark Office.
Reviewers for the Smithsonian See page 160
Smithsonian Enterprises:
Product Development Manager Kealy Wilson
Licensing Manager Ellen Nanney
Vice President of Education and Consumer Products
Brigid Ferraro
Senior Vice President of Education and Consumer Products
Carol LeBlanc

First American Edition, 2014
Published in the United States by DK Publishing
4th floor, 345 Hudson Street, New York, New York 10014

14 15 16 17 18 10 9 8 7 6 5 4 3 2 1
001–192382–08/14

Copyright © 2014 Dorling Kindersley Limited
All rights reserved
Without limiting the rights under copyright reserved above, no part of
this publication may be reproduced, stored in or introduced into a retrieval
system, or transmitted, in any form, or by any means (electronic, mechanical,
photocopying, recording, or otherwise), without the prior written permission
of both the copyright owner and the above publisher of this book.
Published in Great Britain by Dorling Kindersley Limited.

A catalog record for this book is available from the Library of Congress.
ISBN: 978-1-4654-2045-9

DK books are available at special discounts when purchased in bulk for sales
promotions, premiums, fund-raising, or educational use. For details, contact:
DK Publishing Special Markets, 345 Hudson Street, New York, New York 10014
or SpecialSales@dk.com.

Printed and bound in China by Hung Hing

Discover more at www.dk.com

CONTENTS

SPACE

THE EARTH

LIVING WORLD

HISTORY

SCIENCE

HUMAN BODY

Space

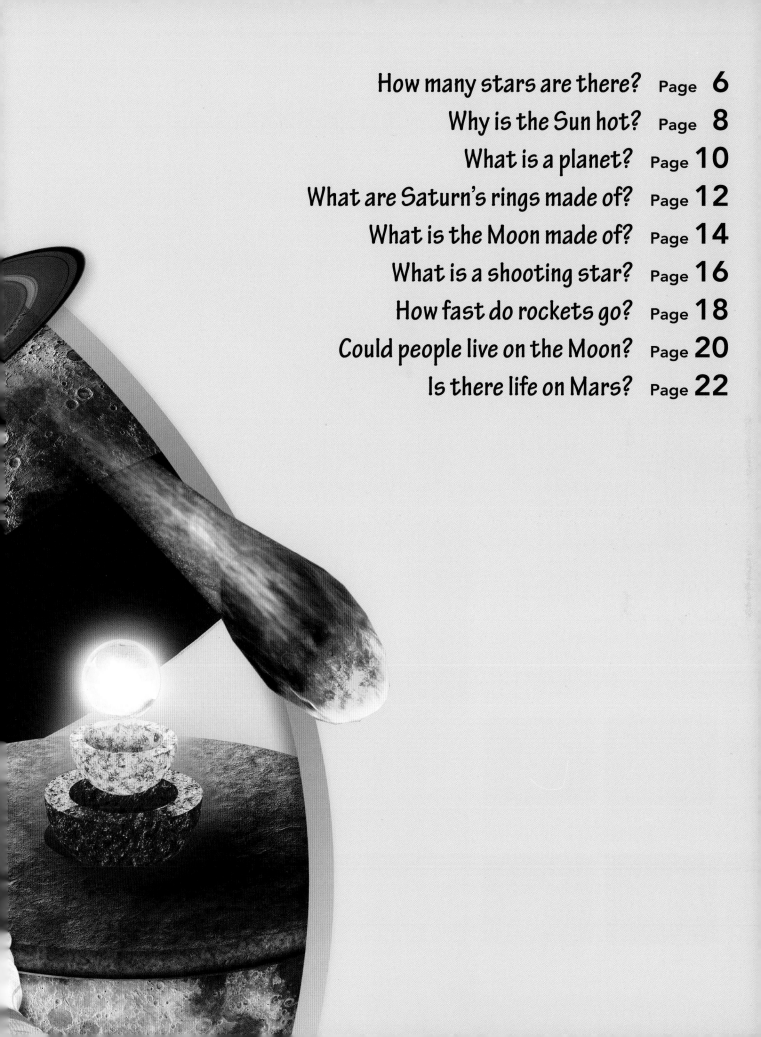

How many stars are there?

Our galaxy, called the Milky Way, has hundreds of billions of stars. There are trillions more galaxies in the universe, each containing countless stars. From the Earth, the Milky Way looks like a band of light in the night sky. If you could fly above our galaxy, it would look like a glittering wheel.

Galaxy shapes

The shape of the Milky Way is called a barred spiral—it has a bar across its center that connects the spiral arms. Galaxies come in different shapes, such as these below.

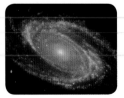
Spiral

Lenticular

Elliptical

Irregular

3 Gas cloud

⭐ 1 Center of the galaxy
A black hole lies hidden in the center of our galaxy. It is called a "black" hole because nothing can escape this point, not even light.

The biggest stars are called supergiants.

olar system 2

The oldest known star is thought to be **13.2 billion years old.**

1 Center of galaxy

5 Dust clouds

4 Spiral arm

5 Dust clouds
The dark areas between the spiral arms are clouds o dust. These are called nebulae

4 Spiral arm
Our galaxy is a spiral shape with four major "arms." Stars, gas, and dust are found in these arms

Quick quiz

 What is the name of our galaxy?

 What is in the center of the galaxy?

 What is the age of the oldest known star?

3 Gas clouds
Our galaxy contains huge clouds of gas. Stars form in the gas clouds, lighting them up.

2 Solar system
Our solar system contains eight planets, around 170 moons, and millions of asteroids and comets. They all orbit (travel around) the star we call the Sun

Why is the Sun hot?

The Sun is a giant ball of different gases. In the Sun's center, which is called the core, these gases produce energy in the form of heat and light. This makes the Sun hot and bright. The energy then travels out through space, reaching Earth in just 8 minutes.

Solar eclipse

A total solar eclipse happens when the Moon comes between the Earth and the Sun, blocking it from view. The sky goes dark and we can see the glowing atmosphere around the Sun called the corona.

Spots on the Sun

Dark patches on the Sun's surface are called sunspots. They are the cooler parts of the surface, but are still incredibly hot.

Hot gas

The Sun is not solid. It is mostly a mixture of two gases called hydrogen and helium.

You could fit about **1 million Earths** inside the Sun.

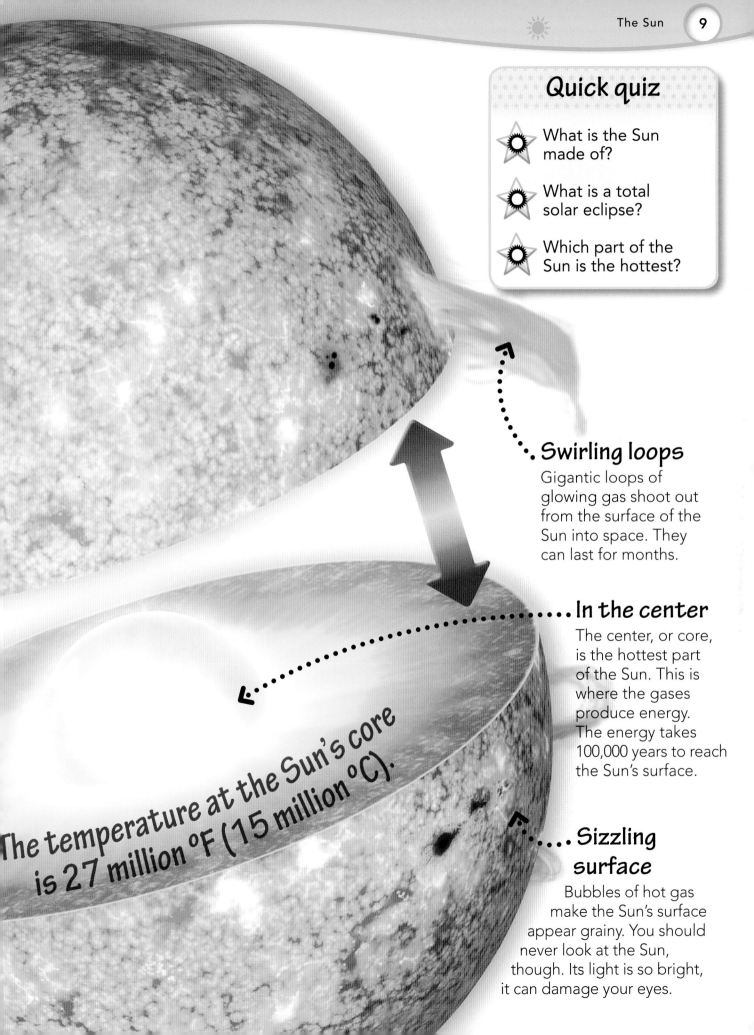

Quick quiz

- What is the Sun made of?
- What is a total solar eclipse?
- Which part of the Sun is the hottest?

Swirling loops

Gigantic loops of glowing gas shoot out from the surface of the Sun into space. They can last for months.

In the center

The center, or core, is the hottest part of the Sun. This is where the gases produce energy. The energy takes 100,000 years to reach the Sun's surface.

The temperature at the Sun's core is 27 million °F (15 million °C).

Sizzling surface

Bubbles of hot gas make the Sun's surface appear grainy. You should never look at the Sun, though. Its light is so bright, it can damage your eyes.

What is a planet?

A planet is a ball-shaped object that orbits (travels around) a star. Eight planets orbit the star we call the Sun. The four planets nearest to the Sun are small and rocky. The four outer planets are larger and made mostly of gas. Together, the Sun and the eight planets make up the solar system.

Quick quiz

 Is Venus bigger or smaller than Earth?

 Why does Mars look red?

 How strong are the winds on Neptune?

The Sun
The Sun is a star at the center of the solar system. Every planet orbits (travels around) it.

Giant Jupiter
Jupiter is the biggest planet—larger than the other seven planets put together.

Mini Mercury
Mercury is the smallest planet and the closest one to the Sun.

Life on Earth
Earth is where we live. It is the only planet in the solar system known to have life.

Spinning backward
Venus is slightly smaller than Earth. It spins in the opposite direction from most of the other planets.

The red planet
Mars is known as the red planet. Its color comes from the iron minerals in the soil on its surface.

Moving around the Sun

Each planet travels around the Sun on its own path, or orbit. The length of time it takes to make one orbit is called a year. Planets also spin as they orbit. The time it takes to make one complete spin is called a day.

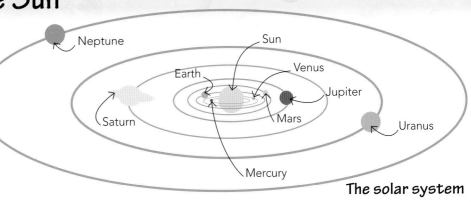

Neptune · Sun · Earth · Venus · Jupiter · Saturn · Mars · Uranus · Mercury

The solar system

10 hours long.

The ringed planet
Saturn is surrounded by visible rings, which are made up of billions of chunks of ice. ••••••

Mercury takes **88 days** to travel around the Sun, but **Neptune** takes **164 years!**

Tilted to the Sun
Uranus is tilted so that its north pole (the top of most planets) is at its side.

Windy Neptune
The winds on Neptune can be nine times stronger than those on Earth.

What are Saturn's rings made of?

The rings of Saturn are made up of billions of pieces of ice. Some are tiny, while others are the size of a house. No one knows how they formed.

Saturn is about 750 times bigger than the Earth.

How many rings?

Saturn has seven main rings around it, along with at least 10 more narrow rings.

Many moons

Scientists have discovered 62 moons orbiting Saturn, and there may be even more. The biggest is called Titan—it is even bigger than the planet Mercury.

Around the middle

The objects in the rings all orbit (travel around) the middle of the planet (its equator).

Squashed shape
Saturn is not a perfect ball-shape. It has a squashed top and bottom and bulges in the middle.

There's a gap
The two widest rings are named A and B; they are the wide gray rings here and are separated by a gap.

A

B

A day on Saturn lasts just **10.5 hours**, but its year is longer than **29 Earth years.**

Quick quiz

 How many main rings does Saturn have?

 What is the name of Saturn's largest moon?

 What are Saturn's two widest rings called?

What is the Moon made of?

The Moon is made of a mixture of rocks and metals. About 4.5 billion years ago, a small planet smashed into the Earth. Lots of chunks broke off and blasted into space. The Moon was made when some of these joined together again.

Solid rock

The mantle is a layer that starts 30 miles (50 km) below the Moon's surface. It is mainly made of solid rock.

Walking on the Moon

The Moon is the only place aside from the Earth where human beings have walked. From 1969 to 1972, a total of 12 astronauts landed on the Moon. They did experiments, took photographs, and brought back samples of rock. This picture is from the very first Moon landing in 1969.

Cratered crust

The Moon's outside, or crust, is made of hard rock. Its surface is covered in very fine, gray dust, and is also scarred with craters. These were made by asteroids that crashed into the Moon during its early life.

Solid iron

The Moon's inner core is a massive ball of hot, solid iron.

Every year, the **Moon** moves 1½ in (4 cm) farther away from the Earth.

Liquid iron

The outer core surrounds the inner core. It is made from hot, liquid iron.

Melting mantle

The inner mantle is partly melted, so some of it is solid and some of it is liquid.

Quick quiz

 How old is the Moon?

 How many people have landed on the Moon?

 Is the center of the Moon liquid or solid?

What is a shooting star?

A shooting star looks like a fast streak of light in the night sky, lasting for just a second. Also called a meteor, it is not a star, but a small piece of rock or metal that burns up as it enters the Earth's atmosphere.

Millions of meteors enter the Earth's atmosphere every day.

Fading fast.....

A meteor's trail fades quickly because the meteor moves very fast—about 45 miles (70 km) per second.

Blazing a trail...........

A trail of light follows the meteor. As it travels, it rubs up against the gas in the atmosphere, making the gas glow.

The Hoba meteorite

Most meteors burn up in the atmosphere, but when one lands on Earth it is called a meteorite. The largest intact meteorite ever found weighs 66 tons (60 metric tons). It was found in Hoba West farm, Namibia, Africa.

Quick quiz

 What is another word for a shooting star?

 How heavy is the Hoba meteorite?

 What is a very bright shooting star called?

Incredibly bright shooting stars are called **fireballs**.

Space fragment ....

Most meteors are very small. They range in size from a pebble down to a grain of sand.

How fast do rockets go?

Rockets travel incredibly fast to reach space. If they didn't, the Earth's gravity would pull them back down again. The powerful Ariane 5 rocket has reached 23,287 mph (37,476 kph)—nearly 6.5 miles (10.5 km) per second!

Launching satellites

Ariane 5's job is to carry satellites into space. Satellites orbit (go around) the Earth, and help to make our internet, television, and cell phones work.

Feeding fuel

A large tank stores the rocket's fuel and feeds it to the engine below.

A rocket can travel at least **30 times faster than** a passenger jet.

Power boost

Extra engines called "solid rocket boosters" give the rocket more power. Once they have done their job, they are released from the rocket and fall into the sea.

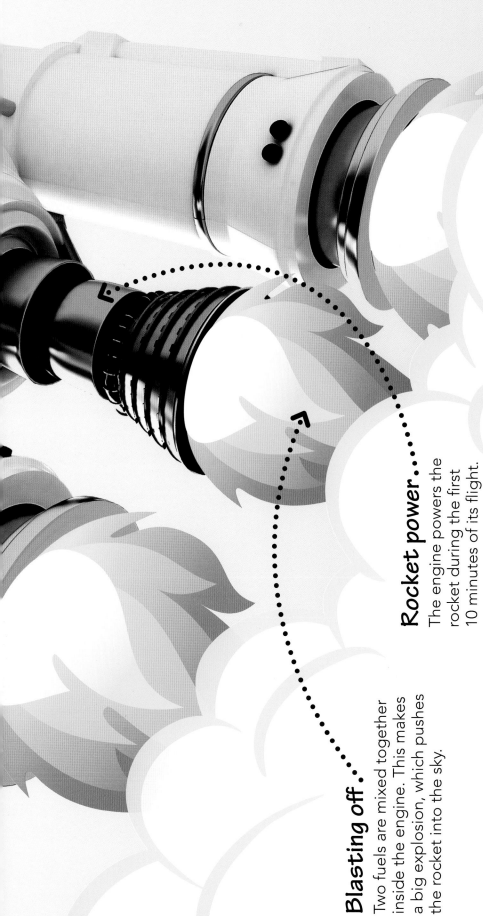

Quick quiz

How fast can Ariane 5 travel?

What does Ariane 5 carry into space?

What are solid rocket boosters for?

Blasting off

Two fuels are mixed together inside the engine. This makes a big explosion, which pushes the rocket into the sky.

Rocket power

The engine powers the rocket during the first 10 minutes of its flight.

Space speed record

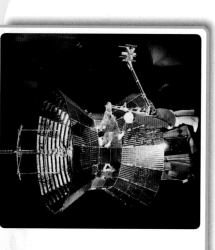

In 1976, the Helios A and Helios B spacecraft reached a speed of 157,000 mph (253,000 kph), or 44 miles (70 km) a second. That is like traveling from London to New York in 1.5 minutes! This speed has never been beaten.

Could people live on the Moon?

There is no air, food, or water on the Moon, so it would be very difficult to live there. When astronauts first walked on the Moon more than 45 years ago, they wore special suits to keep them alive.

Heated hands
The astronaut's gloves had heaters in the fingers because it gets extremely cold on the Moon.

Moon camp
Some people believe that we might be living on the Moon in just 20 years' time, perhaps in a base that looks like the one below. It would have supplies of air, water, and food.

Drilling deep
Astronauts drilled holes in the Moon to put in detectors and to dig up rock samples.

Moon boots
The astronauts' boots were strong to cope with the Moon's rocky surface, which could also get very hot.

Air supply

The astronauts carried oxygen in their backpacks. The oxygen flowed to the helmet so the astronauts could breathe.

Space suits are so complicated they take **over an hour** to put on.

Sun shade

In addition to helping the astronauts to breathe, the helmet protected their eyes from the blinding glare of the Sun.

Keeping cool

The space suit had water running through tubes under the fabric. This made sure the astronauts did not get too hot.

Pressure suit

Astronauts wore a tight rubber suit, called a pressure garment. It had joints so they could move more easily.

Quick quiz

 Why do Moon boots have to be strong?

 How did astronauts breathe on the Moon?

 How long does it take to put on a space suit?

Is there life on Mars?

No life has been found on Mars. However, life might have existed long ago if the conditions were right. A robot called Curiosity has been sent to study the planet to find out if it was warmer and wetter in the past.

Sending signals
There are three antennae on Curiosity. Scientists on Earth use them to communicate with the robot.

Curiosity's top speed is **260 feet per hour** (80 meters per hour)—that's the **speed** of a **tortoise**!

Taking pictures

Curiosity has 17 cameras, which allow scientists on Earth to see whatever it can see. It also has a laser that can turn rocks to dust to find out what they are made of.

Curiosity took more than 8 months to reach Mars.

Working hard

Curiosity's robotic hand has lots of tools. Here it is using a tool to scrape away the surface rock.

On the move

The rover has six tough wheels that help it travel across the bumpy surface.

Quick quiz

 Have we discovered life on Mars?

 How are Curiosity's antennae used?

 How many cameras does Curiosity have?

The Earth

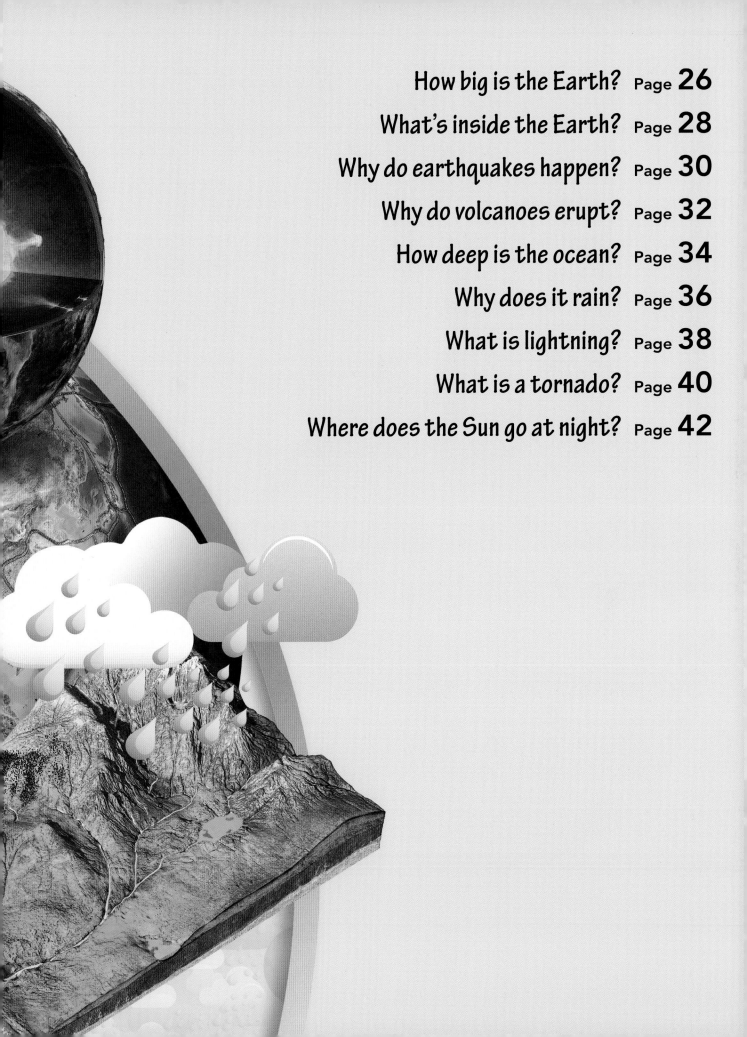

How big is the Earth?

The Earth is a globe (ball), so its widest point is around the middle (also known as the equator). If you tried to walk along the equator, it would take you a year to cover the entire distance of 24,901 miles (40,075 km).

Asia is the **biggest continent**. Around **two-thirds of all the people** in the world live there.

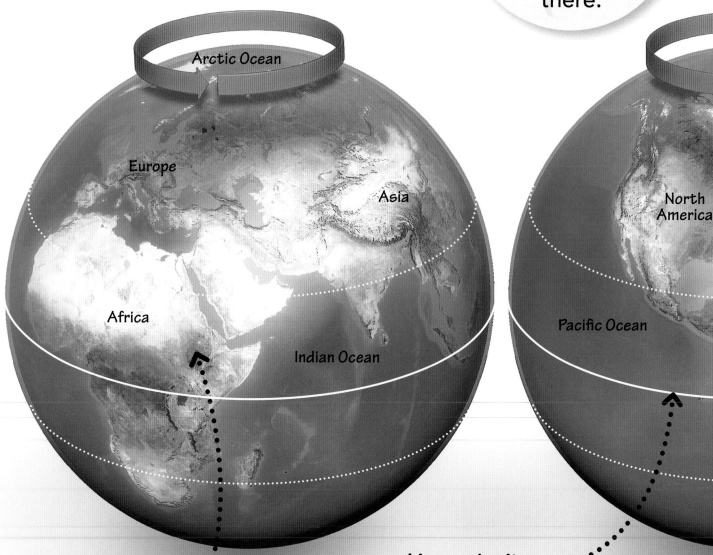

Arctic Ocean

Europe

Asia

North America

Africa

Indian Ocean

Pacific Ocean

Seven continents
Africa is one of seven continents. The others are North America, South America, Europe, Asia, Australasia and Oceania, and Antarctica.

Along the line...
The equator is an imaginary line that runs around the center of the globe. It divides the planet into two halves: the northern hemisphere above the equator, and the southern hemisphere below it.

Continent to country

Continents are huge areas of land. Most continents are divided into countries (except for Antarctica). Countries can be large or small, as shown in this map of South America, where each country is a different color.

Countries of South America

Quick quiz

 How wide is the Earth across the middle?

 What are the seven continents called?

 Does it get cold in the tropics?

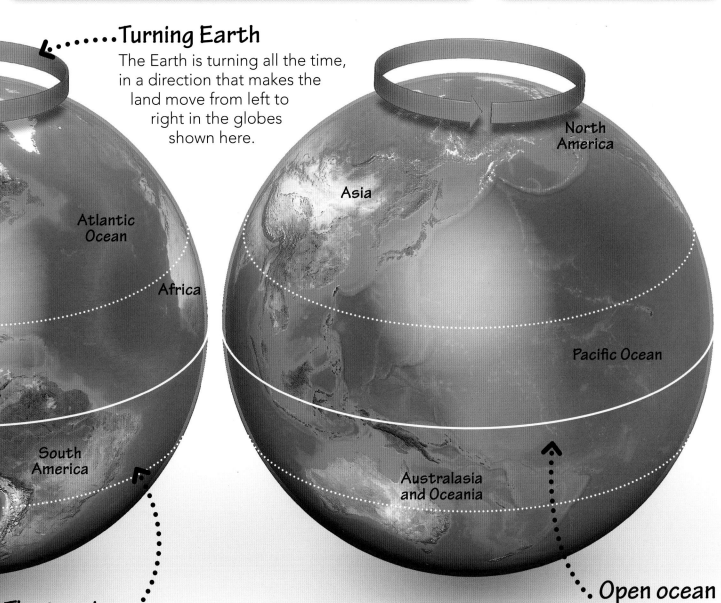

Turning Earth

The Earth is turning all the time, in a direction that makes the land move from left to right in the globes shown here.

Atlantic Ocean

Africa

South America

Asia

North America

Pacific Ocean

Australasia and Oceania

The tropics

The parts of the world that lie on each side of the equator, up to the dotted lines, are known as the tropics. They have two seasons (wet and dry) but stay warm all year round.

Open ocean

Nearly three-quarters of the Earth is covered by open deep water called ocean. It is divided into five main areas: the Pacific, Atlantic, Indian, Arctic, and Southern Antarctic, which is at the bottom of the world.

Outside the Earth

The Earth is surrounded by layers of gases, called the atmosphere. These protect the planet from the Sun's rays and give us the air we need to breathe.

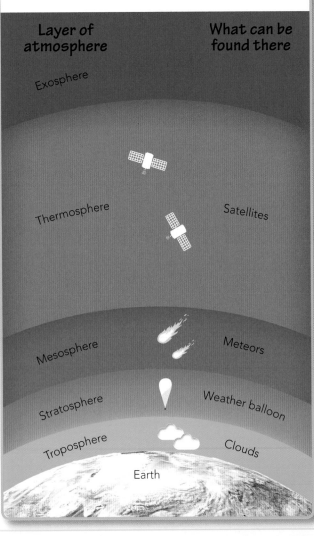

Layer of atmosphere	What can be found there
Exosphere	
Thermosphere	Satellites
Mesosphere	Meteors
Stratosphere	Weather balloon
Troposphere	Clouds

Earth

The Earth was formed 4.5 billion years ago.

What's inside the Earth?

Planet Earth is a giant rocky ball spinning in space. We live on its thin outer layer, called the crust, but there are more layers on the inside. At the very center is a hot, solid, metal core.

Crust

Mantle

Outer core

Inner core

Rocky crust

The Earth's rocky outer surface is called the crust. It forms the ocean floor under the sea and the continents, where we live.

Molten mantle

The mantle is a thick layer of hot rock. This rock is so hot that some of it melts and forms a liquid called magma. Magma moves around in the mantle very slowly.

Liquid outer core

The outer core is a hot, liquid mixture of two metals called iron and nickel, and a mineral called sulfur.

Solid middle

The Earth's inner core is a hot, solid mixture of iron and nickel.

The temperature of the **Earth's inner core** is **10,800°F (6,000°C).**

Quick quiz

 Where is the Earth's atmosphere?

 What do we call the Earth's outer layer?

 Which layer is made of hot, solid metal?

Why do earthquakes happen?

The Earth's crust is like a huge jigsaw puzzle, made up of pieces called plates. These plates are moving very slowly, all the time. When two plates rub against each other, the pressure can cause earthquakes, making the ground shake.

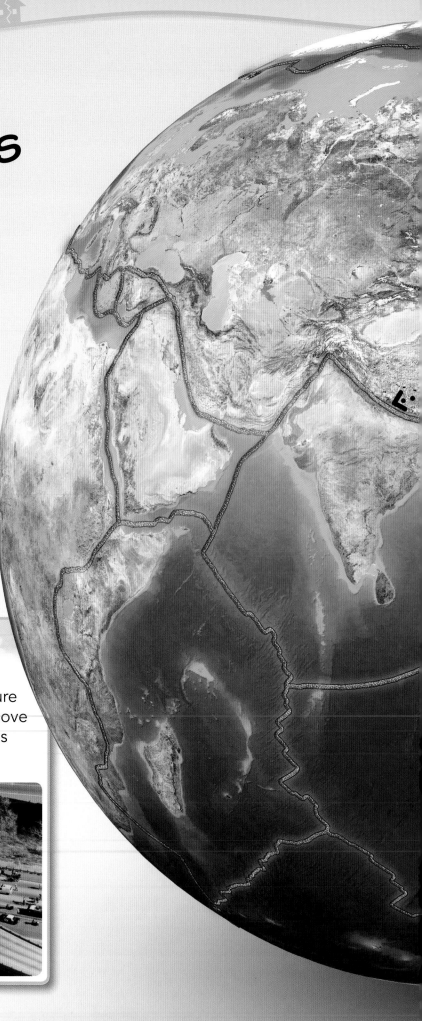

Earthquake power

Earthquakes can be measured on the Richter scale. Weak earthquakes measure less than 3.5 on the scale, but those above 7 are strong enough to topple buildings and make roads and bridges collapse.

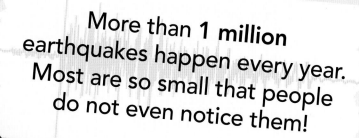

More than **1 million** earthquakes happen every year. Most are so small that people do not even notice them!

Pacific quake

In 2011, a huge earthquake took place in Japan. It began in the Pacific Ocean, where one plate moved beneath another.

Making mountains

The Himalayan mountains were formed when two plates pushed together, making the ground rise up in huge peaks. These plates are still moving against each other, which often causes earthquakes in this region.

Giant waves

In 2004, an earthquake under the Indian Ocean caused a tsunami—an enormous wave. The waves washed ashore and caused destruction in 14 different countries.

Quick quiz

 What causes earthquakes?

 How are earthquakes measured?

 How many earthquakes happen each year?

Why do volcanoes erupt?

Volcanoes can erupt when pressure deep underground forces hot, liquid rock (called magma) from inside the Earth up to the surface. An eruption blasts out clouds of ash and molten (melted) rock into the air around it.

Escape route
Magma rises up a main pipe from deep within the Earth's crust and is forced toward the surface.

Trapped underground
Pools of magma build up deep underground. This hot, liquid rock comes from the Earth's interior.

Quick quiz

★ Where does magma come from?

★ Why are volcanoes often cone-shaped?

★ How many volcanoes erupt each year?

Rivers of fire

An erupting volcano can produce fountains of red hot lava that run down its sides burning everything in their path. When an eruption blows off the top of the volcano, lava may also form a lake in the crater that is left behind.

Ash clouds

Thick clouds of burning hot ash are blasted up to several miles into the Earth's atmosphere.

Flowing lava

At the Earth's surface, magma is called lava, which flows down the sides of the volcano. The lava cools in layers, often with ash in between, that gives the volcano its cone shape.

The temperature of lava is a scorching 1,800°F (1,000°C).

Around **50–70 volcanoes** erupt in the world each year and about **20 volcanoes** are erupting right now.

Quick quiz

 What is an ocean trench?

 Which zone has the most sea life?

 How do scientists reach the ocean floor?

How deep is the ocean?

The deepest part of the ocean is 7 miles (11 km) under water. Just like on dry land, the ocean floor has mountains and valleys. The deepest parts are called trenches. Not much lives at these cold, dark depths, but there is much more life in the zones above.

0 ft (0 m)   650 ft (200 m)   3,300 ft (1,000 m)

Corals

Mackerel

Sponges

Starfish

Seaweeds

Bluntnose sixgill shark

Jellyfish

Sponges

Combjelly

Scuba diver

Whale shark

Tuna

Sperm whale

Squid

Sunlit sea

The top zone is the sunlit zone, where sunlight reaches 650 ft (200 m) down into the clear, blue water. Most sea life lives here, where there is plenty of food. Scuba divers can safely explore to depths of around 165 ft (50 m).

Murky twilight

The next level, down to 3,300 ft (1,000 m), is called the twilight zone. Fewer fishes and sea creatures live here, where the sea is darker and colder.

Dark waters

The dark zone drops from 3,300–13,000 ft (1,000–4,000 m). Only deep-sea fishes and animals can survive in these cold waters, where there is less chance of finding food.

13,000 ft
(4,000 m)

36,000 ft
(11,000 m)

Deep-sea anglerfish

...gfish

Black swallower

Cusk eel

Submarine

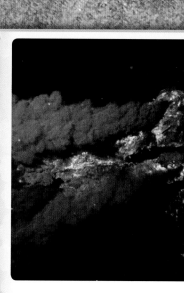

Chimneys under the sea

Water heated by hot rocks can spring out of the sea bed through large cracks in the Earth's crust. Grains of minerals in the water make it look like smoke. The grains pile up and quickly harden into chimneylike towers up to 200 ft (60 m) high.

The cusk eel is the world's **deepest living fish,** surviving at **26,000 ft (8,000 m)** below the surface.

Deepest depths

Little is known about the deepest, darkest areas of the ocean, which stretch down to almost 36,000 ft (11,000 m). These are zones that we are only just beginning to explore for signs of life.

Why does it rain?

The clouds in the sky are made up of tiny water droplets, which rise into the air when the Sun heats the sea. The droplets get larger and heavier, then fall to the ground as rain. This water runs into rivers, which flow from the land back to the sea. This never-ending journey is called the water cycle.

2 Drifting clouds

Winds blow the clouds over the land. When the clouds drift into cooler air, the tiny water droplets start to join together to form larger, heavier raindrops.

1 Rising water

The Sun heats the sea and turns the water into invisible water vapor, which rises into the air. The warm water vapor cools into millions of tiny water droplets, which form clouds.

3 Falling rain

When the water droplets get too large and heavy, they fall as rain. Cold air above high mountains often freezes the water, which then falls as hail or snow.

Raindrops fall at speeds of **5–22 mph** (8–35 kph).

4 Flowing rivers

The water runs into streams and rivers, which flow downhill to lower ground. Some rivers empty into lakes. Others carry the water back to the sea, where the cycle starts all over again.

Quick quiz

- What happens when clouds cool?

- Where does rain often fall as snow?

- How does rainwater travel back to the sea?

What is lightning?

Lightning is a bright flash of electricity produced by some powerful storms. This happens when the raindrops in clouds turn to ice and knock together, creating electricity. When too much of this electricity builds up, it is released in the form of giant sparks called lightning.

Superstorms

Thunderstorms are made up of several storm clouds joined together. They can stretch as wide as 20 miles (30 km) across.

Noisy flash

A flash of lightning is burning hot. It heats up the air, which expands very quickly and produces a noisy crash of thunder. You see the lightning before you hear the thunder because light travels faster than sound.

Lightning flashes are a scorching **54,000°F (30,000°C)—five times hotter** than the surface of the Sun.

Fearsome forks

Forked lighting is the name for lightning that appears as jagged lines of light split into several branches.

Ground strikes

Cloud-to-ground lightning strikes tall things, such as trees and buildings. The powerful electric current can cause great damage and set things on fire.

Lightning strikes last a fraction of a second.

Quick quiz

 How hot is a flash of lightning?

 Why does lightning create thunder?

What is sheet lightning?

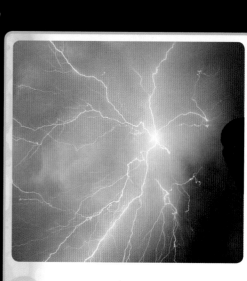

Sparking clouds

Not all lightning strikes reach the ground. Cloud-to-cloud lightning happens when huge sparks of electricity leap across the sky from one storm cloud to another. These huge flashes of light are known as sheet lightning.

What is a tornado?

Tornadoes are powerful, swirling, spinning winds that sometimes form beneath a storm cloud. Wherever they touch land, tornadoes sweep across the ground, leaving behind a trail of destruction. A tornado can last for just a few seconds or for more than an hour.

2 Spinning air

As warm air meets cool, swirling air high in the cloud, it starts to spin. Soon the air lower down is spinning, too.

Whirling water

When a whirling air mass passes over warm, shallow seas, it sucks up water into a funnel of air that is called a waterspout. A waterspout may have lower wind speeds than a tornado, but it can last far longer.

3 Cloud column

More of the surrounding air is pulled in and the growing tornado spins even faster. It then forms a column of twisting cloud that reaches the ground.

1 Stormy weather

Dark, violent storm clouds build up where warm, moist air rising from the land meets cool, dry air in the sky.

Around **1,000 tornadoes** a year strike in the United States, mostly in an area called **Tornado Alley.**

Tornadoes spin at speeds of up to 200 mph (320 kph).

4 Blown away

The strong, whirling winds suck up and destroy anything lying in their path. A tornado can tear up trees, buildings, and cars, then drop them many miles away after it has weakened.

Quick quiz

 How long can tornadoes last?

 What is a waterspout?

 How fast do tornadoes spin?

Where does the Sun go at night?

The Sun doesn't move anywhere—it just disappears because we live on a planet that is always spinning. Every evening the part of the planet where you live turns away from the Sun and you can see the blackness of space. The Earth keeps spinning through the night. Daylight returns when your part of the Earth turns back to face the Sun.

Constant sunlight

The Sun is our closest star and it lies at the center of the solar system. The Sun's rays give our planet constant heat and light, which are vital to all life.

Light of day

This half of the planet is facing toward the Sun, so it is in daylight and the Sun can be seen in the sky.

Spinning Earth

The Earth spins from west to east, or left to right in this book. Since this part of the Earth moves right (east), the Sun will set and night will begin.

Quick quiz

 What is the name of our closest star?

 When is it daylight on Earth?

 Why does the Moon shine in the sky?

....Dark nights

This half of the planet is facing away from the Sun and in shadow, so it is dark. People in the cities have turned on their lights so they can get around safely in the darkness.

We don't feel it, but the Earth is **spinning** at a speed of **1,040 mph** (1,675 kph). That's **17 miles (28 km) every minute.**

Earth takes 24 hours to make one turn.

Moonlight

The Moon is a ball of rock with no light of its own. It shines because it reflects sunlight— even during the night.

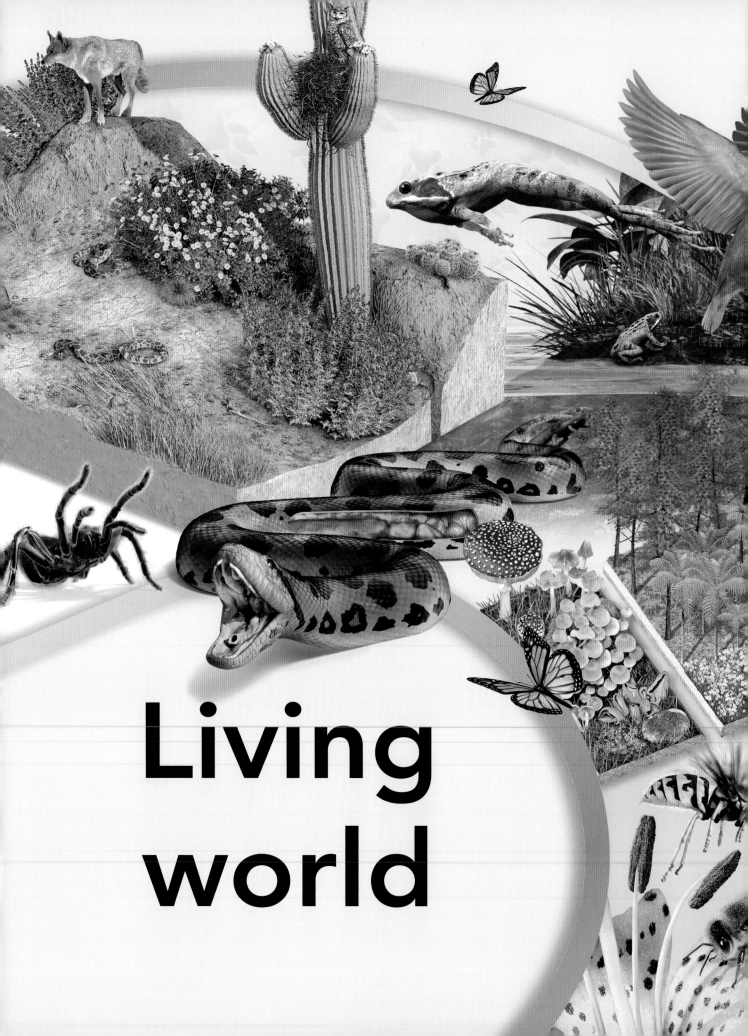

Living world

Are plants alive?

Just like animals, plants are living things; they are able to grow, reproduce (have "babies"), and die. Plants are just one of five main groups, or kingdoms, of living things in the world.

Maritime pine trees

Smallest living things

Bacteria are too small to see without a microscope. They are made up of just one cell—the tiny building blocks that make up all living things. People have trillions of cells.

Fly agaric

Pink waxcap

Protists

Bacteria

Sulfur tuft

Hare's ear

Lichen

Devil's matchstick

Single cells

Another group of tiny living thing lives in water or in soil. Some make food like plants; others take in food like animals.

Fungi

Mushrooms and toadstools are part of the group called fungi. They feed on dead plants and animals.

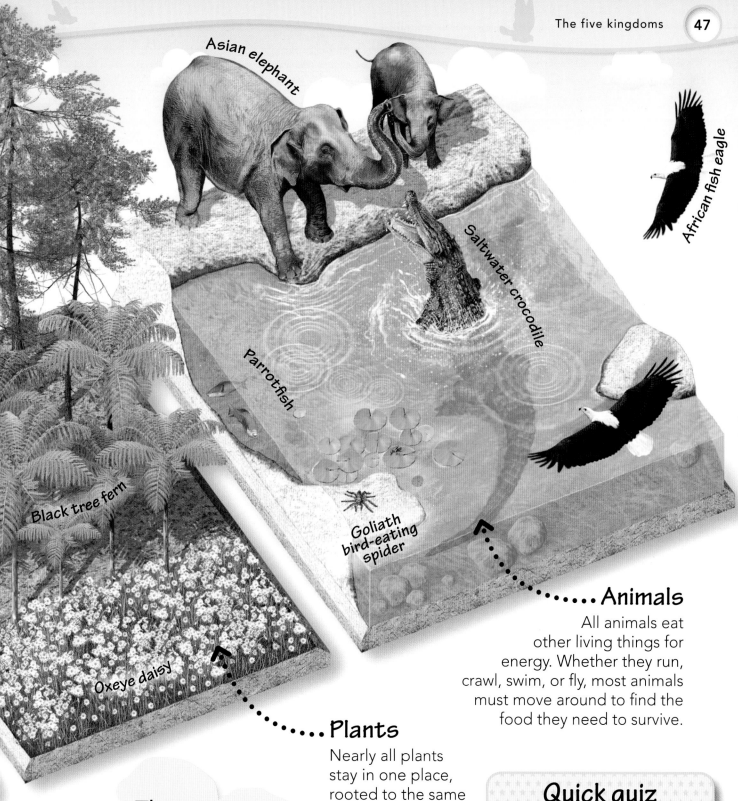

Asian elephant

African fish eagle

Saltwater crocodile

Parrotfish

Black tree fern

Goliath bird-eating spider

Oxeye daisy

Animals
All animals eat other living things for energy. Whether they run, crawl, swim, or fly, most animals must move around to find the food they need to survive.

Plants
Nearly all plants stay in one place, rooted to the same spot. Most plants use sunlight, water, air, and their green leaves to make their own food.

There are around **289,000 different kinds of plant** living in the world.

Quick quiz

 How many cells are bacteria made up of?

 What do most plants use to make food?

 What do animals eat for energy?

Why are leaves green?

Leaves are green because they contain a green chemical called chlorophyll. Plants use chlorophyll to absorb sunlight so they can make food. This process is called photosynthesis. Photosynthesis takes place during the day when the Sun is out.

Sunlight

Sunlight

Carbon dioxide

1 Carbon dioxide in

During the day, leaves take in carbon dioxide from the air, water from the tree's roots, and sunlight. They mix them together to make sugar and oxygen.

Oxygen

2 Oxygen out

The leaves release the oxygen they have made, because they do not need it, and store the sugar for food.

Quick quiz

- What is photosynthesis?

- What does a tree's roots take in?

- Why does a tree take in oxygen?

Spreading out........

A tree's roots may reach deep down or spread far and wide to gather as much water as possible.

Losing water

The surface of a leaf has tiny openings, called stomata. They open to let gases in and out, and water escapes as a gas called water vapor. More water flows to the leaf to replace the water vapor. This keeps water flowing through the whole plant.

Stomata

Cells

Water vapor

Oxygen

3 Oxygen in

Plants absorb oxygen at night. They use it to turn the food they've made during the day into energy.

4 Carbon dioxide out

At night, plants release carbon dioxide because they don't need it to make food.

Carbon dioxide

Watery roots

Trees absorb (take in) water from the soil through their roots. The water travels up the trunk to the branches and leaves.

The food that plants make is a kind of **sugar** called **glucose**.

Why do plants have flowers?

A plant's flowers help it to reproduce (make more plants). Flowers attract insects and some birds and bats. These animals carry a grainy dust called pollen from one flower to another. Flowers use this pollen to produce seeds.

Sticky stigma

Visiting insects may rub against the stigma, leaving pollen grains behind. Each grain grows a tube that travels down the style to the ovary.

Stigma

Style

Anther

Pollen store

Anthers produce the tiny grains of pollen that stick to visiting insects.

Pretty petals

The color, shape, and size of a flower's petals, and the smell of the flower, attract insects.

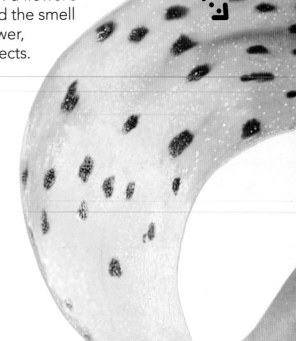

Spreading seeds

A plant needs to spread its seeds so that new plants can grow. Many plants make seeds inside fruit. Animals eat the fruit and scatter these seeds in their droppings. Some other flowers, such as dandelions, produce very light seeds that blow away in the wind.

Collecting pollen

Insects such as bees visit flowers to drink nectar and collect pollen. As the insects crawl on the flower, some pollen grains from the anthers stick to their bodies and legs. When the bees visit other flowers, this pollen rubs off on their stigmas.

Anther

Anther

Pollen

Sweet food

Nectar is made at the bottom of the flower. Insects crawl inside to reach the sweet, sugary liquid.

The Queen of the Andes is a South American plant that flowers after 80–150 years and then dies.

Ovary

Inside the flower...

The ovary contains the plant's eggs. Pollen that collects on the stigma comes down the style to join with the eggs and grow into seeds.

Quick quiz

 Which part of a flower produces the pollen?

 Why do insects visit flowers?

 Where is nectar made?

How many animals are there in the world?

There are trillions of individual animals living in the world—far too many to count! However, scientists think there are about 8.7 million different species (kinds) of animal on the planet. They sort animal species with similar features into different groups.

Emu

Giant tortoise

Chameleon

Caecilian

Bottlenose dolphin

Giraffe

Macaw

Owl

Crocodile

Lion

Peafowl

King penguin

Green iguana

Swan

Hare

Scarlet ibis

Bald eagle

Gray wolf

Mammals

Chimpanzee

Red kangaroo

Birds

Mammals

Most mammals give birth to live young and all feed their babies on milk.

Birds

Birds have feathers and most of them can fly using their wings. They produce young by laying eggs.

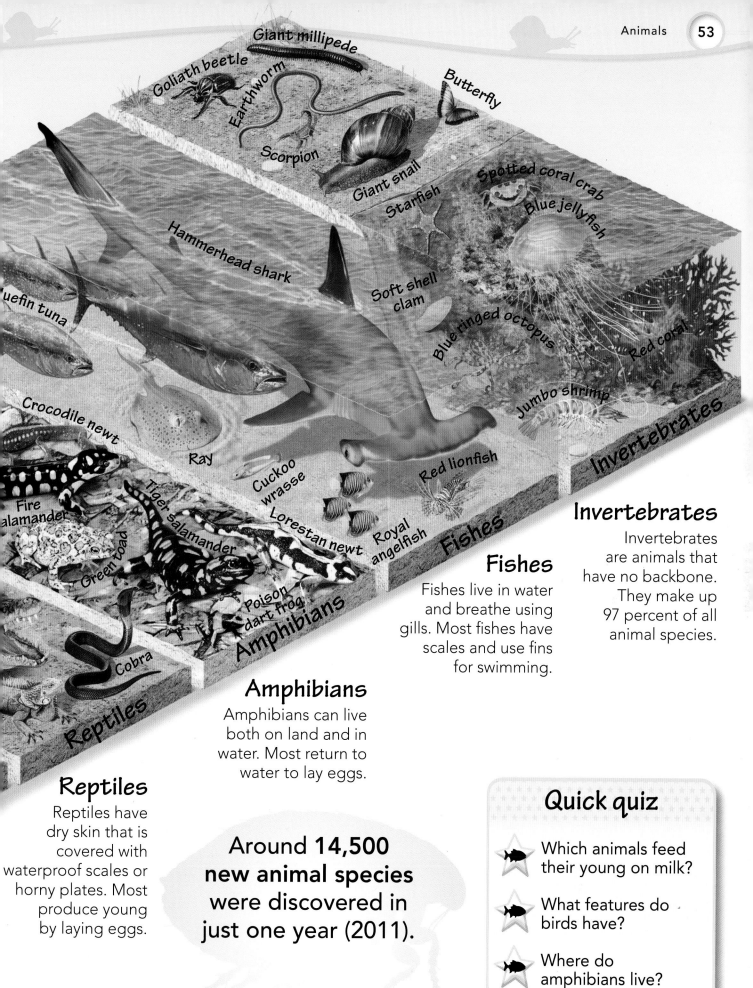

Giant millipede

Goliath beetle

Earthworm

Butterfly

Scorpion

Giant snail

Starfish

Spotted coral crab

Blue jellyfish

Hammerhead shark

Soft shell clam

Blue ringed octopus

uefin tuna

Red coral

Crocodile newt

Jumbo shrimp

Invertebrates

Ray

Cuckoo wrasse

Red lionfish

Fire alamander

Lorestan newt

Royal angelfish

Fishes

Tiger salamander

Green toad

Poison dart frog

Amphibians

Cobra

Reptiles

Invertebrates

Invertebrates are animals that have no backbone. They make up 97 percent of all animal species.

Fishes

Fishes live in water and breathe using gills. Most fishes have scales and use fins for swimming.

Amphibians

Amphibians can live both on land and in water. Most return to water to lay eggs.

Reptiles

Reptiles have dry skin that is covered with waterproof scales or horny plates. Most produce young by laying eggs.

Around **14,500 new animal species** were discovered in just one year (2011).

Quick quiz

Which animals feed their young on milk?

What features do birds have?

Where do amphibians live?

Why do lions have fur?

Lions belong to the group of animals called mammals. These animals have hair on their bodies to help keep them warm. Some mammals, such as human beings, are less hairy, but most have a covering of fur all over their bodies.

Lion cubs stay with their mother for up to 30 months.

Quick quiz

 Which group of animals has a covering of hair?

 What do mother lions feed to their cubs?

 Why are lions hard to see in the grass?

Unusual mammals

There are around 5,000 different types of mammal. A few are unusual, because they don't give birth to fully developed babies.

Duck-billed platypus
This mammal lays eggs. When the babies hatch, they feed on their mother's milk.

Kangaroo
Newborn kangaroos grow inside their mother's pouch. They feed on their mother's milk until they are strong enough to live outside the pouch.

Sharp teeth
Lions and other meat-eating mammals have pointed teeth for gripping and killing prey and sharp teeth for slicing up meat.

Hard to spot
The lions' sandy-colored fur coats blend in with the dry grass. This helps them to creep up on prey. Female lions hunt together to chase down animals, such as zebras.

Only **male lions** have a thick **shaggy mane** of long hair.

Raising families
Female lions, like most mammals, give birth to live babies and produce milk for feeding their young. These lion cubs will drink milk from their mother's teats for the first few months of their lives.

How do birds fly?

Birds fly by flapping their wings. Their bodies are ideal for flight because they are light and shaped to cut through the air. Birds like the kingfisher can hover in midair by beating their wings very fast, while others glide on the wind by stretching their wings wide.

Birds are the only living animals with feathers.

Feathery wings

The kingfisher has large wing feathers for flying. When it flaps, the bird pushes these feathers through the air to move forward and upward.

The fastest flappers are tiny **bee hummingbirds.** They can beat their wings **80 times a second.**

Mighty muscles

The kingfisher's large chest muscles help to power the beating of its wings when it is flying.

Quick quiz

 Which feathers are used for flying?

 Why do birds have large chest muscles?

 Why do birds need light bones?

Bony support

The tips of the kingfisher's tiny wing bones are stuck together to make them stronger.

Folding wings

The kingfisher uses its wing muscles to fold its wings or to alter their shape. This helps the bird to change direction when it is flying.

Smooth shape

A top layer of small feathers gives the kingfisher its smooth shape.

Light bones

Flying uses a lot of energy but birds have light bodies to make flight easier. Their biggest bones are hollow to save weight and their bones have strong supports to stop them from breaking.

Hollow spaces in the bones save weight.

Supports make the bone strong.

Tail feathers

The bird's tail feathers can spread out to help it slow down for landing.

Are all snakes poisonous?

Snakes are not poisonous—they are venomous (they are not deadly if eaten, but can kill prey by biting and injecting it with venom, a kind of poison). However, not all of them kill their prey with venom. Some snakes, such as the enormous green anaconda, coil around their victims and squeeze them to death.

Heavyweight

The anaconda's large, heavy body makes it a slow mover on land, especially after eating. It can take the snake days to digest a big meal.

Big stretch

The anaconda can stretch its jawbones apart, so that it can eat large animals whole.

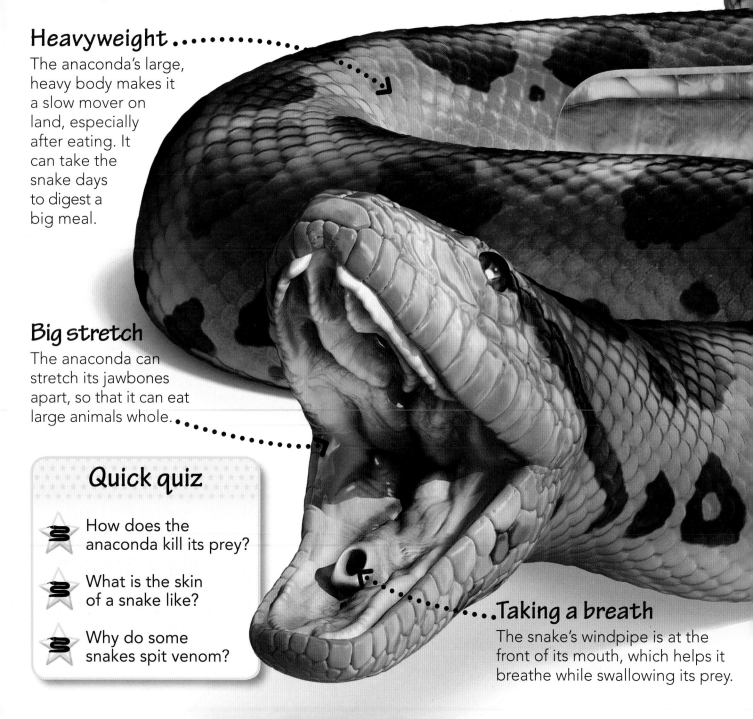

Quick quiz

★ How does the anaconda kill its prey?

★ What is the skin of a snake like?

★ Why do some snakes spit venom?

Taking a breath

The snake's windpipe is at the front of its mouth, which helps it breathe while swallowing its prey.

Scaly skin

All snakes have dry skin covered in scales. These help them to glide over the ground and provide grip to climb trees.

Skinny insides

The snake's stomach and other organs are long and thin to fit inside its body. The stomach stretches to help it digest large prey.

Liver

Stomach

Gall bladder

Spleen

Small intestine

Spitting snakes

Many snakes kill their prey by biting them with their venomous fangs. Some kinds of cobra can spray venom up to 10 ft (3 m) to scare off enemies.

One **deadly bite** from an Australian inland taipan contains enough venom to kill **100 people**.

How do tadpoles turn into frogs?

Tadpoles hatch from frogs' eggs laid in water. As they grow, tadpoles slowly start to change shape. They grow legs and lose their tails as they develop into young frogs that can live on land. This change from tadpole to frog is called metamorphosis.

The goliath frog is the **largest in the world**. It can grow up to **13 in (32 cm) long.**

1 Hatching eggs

Female frogs lay jellylike clumps of eggs called frogspawn in ponds and rivers. The eggs hatch into tiny, swimming tadpoles.

2 Living in water

Tadpoles spend their first weeks of life in water. They swim using their long tails and breathe using gills, like fishes.

3 Growing legs

After two months, tadpoles grow two back legs. They start to feed a lot, nibbling on algae in the water.

Animal groups

Frogs, newts, and wormlike creatures called caecilians make up the three groups of animals called amphibians. Like frogs, the young of these animals hatch from eggs and look very different from the full-grown adults.

Frog   Newt   Caecilian

5 Living on land

By four months, frogs are fully grown, with strong back legs, which help them to swim, climb, and leap on land. Adult frogs will return to the water to find a mate and lay eggs.

4 Breathing air

After three months, tadpoles grow lungs to breathe air from the surface of the water. They also grow front legs and their tails start to shrivel up.

Quick quiz

⭐ Where do frogs lay their eggs?

⭐ When do tadpoles grow back legs?

⭐ When do tadpoles lose their tails?

How can fishes breathe under water?

Living things have to breathe, because they need oxygen to survive. People use their lungs to take in oxygen from the air, but fishes have organs called gills at the sides of their heads that allow them to get oxygen from the water.

More than **32,500 different kinds** of fish live in the world's **rivers, lakes, and oceans.**

1 Water flows in
When a fish opens its mouth, water rushes in and flows toward its gills.

Water in

Water out

Water out

2 Water filter
The water is pushed through bony spines inside the fish's head called gill rakers. These clean the water and stop sand or mud from getting through.

3 Feathery filaments
The water then flows out of the fish's mouth through its gills, which contain feathery strands called filaments. These filaments take the oxygen from the water and pass it into the fish's blood.

Slippery scales

Most fishes have a smooth body covered with scales. These help to protect the fish's body.

Fishes first appeared on the Earth 500 million years ago.

Quick quiz

 Where are the gills on a fish's body?

 What do the feathery filaments do?

 Can sea mammals breathe under water?

Breathing through blowholes

Not all sea creatures breathe using gills. Whales are mammals with lungs and so they must swim to the surface to breathe air. Whales draw in air and blow it out through blowholes on the top of their heads.

What's the biggest spider?

The world's biggest spider is the goliath bird-eating tarantula. It is the heaviest spider, at 6.2 oz (175 g). With its legs outstretched, it is 11 in (28 cm) wide. This giant, hairy spider hunts at night, waiting to pounce on passing prey.

There are more than **42,000 different kinds** of spider.

Bristly body

The hairlike bristles on the tarantula's body are used to feel vibrations. This helps tarantulas sense things around them and also makes up for their poor eyesight.

Body case

Every spider has a hard, outer layer called an exoskeleton to protect it. As it gets bigger, the spider pulls out of its exoskeleton and grows a new one.

Quick quiz

★ What is a spider's exoskeleton?

★ How do tarantulas poison their prey?

★ How many legs do spiders have?

Gripping claws

A tarantula has a pair of claws at the end of each leg that it uses to grip when climbing.

Catching prey

Many spiders trap flying insects by spinning a web made from strong silk threads. The spider then wraps its prey in sticky threads so that it can't move. Spiders can't eat solid food, so they inject their prey with special juices. These turn their meal into a liquid, which the spiders then suck up.

Bendy legs

All spiders have eight legs and each leg has six joints. This makes them very nimble.

Fearsome fangs

Tarantulas have two large fangs that inject venom (poison) into their prey. They feed mainly on insects, but also eat mice, frogs, small lizards, and snakes.

How do caterpillars turn into butterflies?

A caterpillar starts its life by hatching from an egg. The caterpillar feeds and grows, and then wraps its body inside a hard case called a pupa. Next, the caterpillar completely changes shape in a process called metamorphosis. Finally, it leaves the pupa as an adult butterfly with wings.

③ Wrapping up

The pupa wraps around the caterpillar. Inside the pupa, the caterpillar's body starts to change shape.

② Hanging on

When fully grown, the caterpillar attaches itself to a twig using a silken thread. It sheds its skin again and its new skin hardens into a tough case, called a pupa or chrysalis.

① Eating leaves

A caterpillar, or butterfly larva, hatches from an egg. It eats mostly leaves and quickly outgrows its skin, which it sheds several times.

There are around **20,000 types** of butterfly in the world.

Quick quiz

 What do caterpillars eat?

 What happens inside the chrysalis?

 Where do butterflies lay eggs?

Growing up

Many young insects, such as flies and beetles, look very different from full-grown adults. Like caterpillars, they also start life as crawling larvae and turn into flying adults inside a hard case called a pupa.

Young fly larvae (or maggots)

Adult blue bottle fly

Young ladybug larvae

Adult ladybugs

4 Changing shape

The chrysalis changes color as the caterpillar changes into a butterfly.

5 Splitting open

Finally, the chrysalis breaks open and the adult butterfly crawls out. Its large, crumpled wings have to expand and dry before it can fly.

Some butterflies fly 2,000 miles (3,200 km) to lay eggs.

6 Flying away

The butterfly flies away to visit flowers and feed on their sweet nectar. After mating, female butterflies lay their eggs on plants and the life cycle starts again!

Why do wasps sting?

Only female wasps and only some species of wasp can sting. Social wasps (which live in groups) may sting to defend themselves or their nests if they are in danger. Solitary wasps (which live alone) also use their sting to kill or stun their prey.

A sting in the tail

A wasp's sting injects venom (poison) into its prey. Wasps can curl the back part of their bodies under and forward to use the sting.

Insect defense

Not all insects have a sting to defend themselves. Assassin bugs can spit venom (poison) at an attacker from up to 1 ft (30 cm) away. They also kill prey by biting it and injecting it with venom. Sometimes they work as a team to overpower prey much bigger than themselves.

Assassin bug

Warning stripes

These black and yellow stripes warn other animals that the wasp is dangerous.

Barbs and claws

Wasps have sharp barbs on their legs. At the end of their legs, claws help them to grip and carry prey.

Quick quiz

 Why do wasps have stripes?

 What is a wasp's antennae used for?

 How many lenses are in a wasp's eye?

A wasp can **sting many times**, but a bee can sting only once.

Scent detector

The stalks on a wasp's head are called antennae. It uses them to detect scents and tastes.

Super eyesight

A wasp's eyes are made up of thousands of tiny lenses. They make the wasp very good at spotting moving objects.

Pinching jaws

The wasp's jaws have hard, sharp edges. They work like scissors, pinching together to cut into and mash up prey.

Do animals have houses?

Many animals—from birds in trees to animals in the seas—create burrows, dens, and nests in all kinds of places. These homes are normally built as a safe place for them to live, where they can lay eggs or give birth to babies. To keep their families safe, some animals, such as beavers, build their homes in very clever ways.

Beaver builder
The beaver cuts down trees with its strong teeth and builds a dam across a stream using tree branches, mud, and weeds.

Secret entrance
The dam blocks enough water to make a pond where the beaver builds a winter home called a lodge. The lodge has a secret underwater entrance.

Rocks and gravel
Below the water, the beaver piles up rocks and gravel to make the dam very strong.

The **longest beaver dam** ever seen was **2,800 ft (850 m)** long!

Termite cities

Termites are tiny insects that live in large groups called colonies. Some kinds of termite build huge nests several yards high. At the center of the nest is the chamber where the termite queen lives. She lays thousands of eggs every day and these are taken to other parts of the nest to be cared for by blind "worker" termites.

Model of a large termite nest

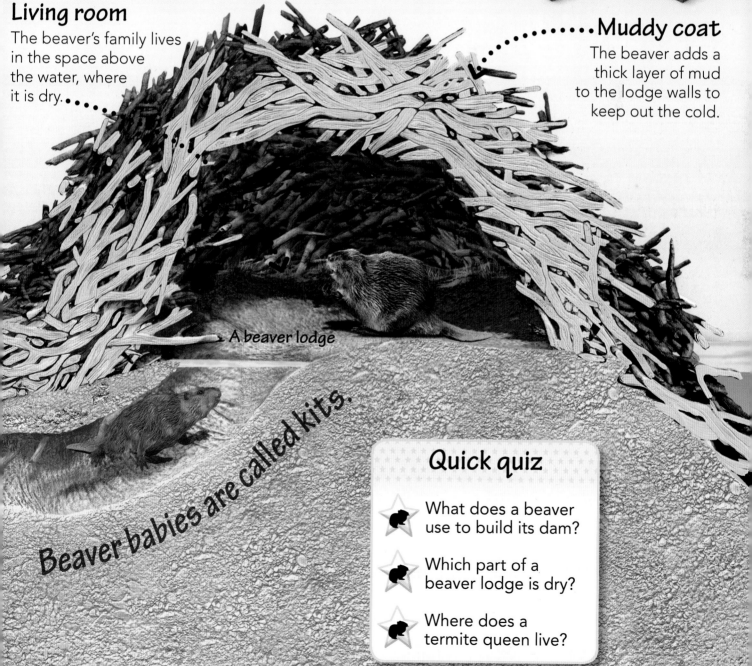

Living room
The beaver's family lives in the space above the water, where it is dry.

Muddy coat
The beaver adds a thick layer of mud to the lodge walls to keep out the cold.

A beaver lodge

Beaver babies are called kits.

Quick quiz

★ What does a beaver use to build its dam?

★ Which part of a beaver lodge is dry?

★ Where does a termite queen live?

Can anything survive in the desert?

Deserts are areas in which very little rain falls. Some are sandy and rocky places with little life. Others, such as the deserts of North America, get more rain, so more plants can grow there. Animals live in deserts, too. They have special ways of finding food and keeping cool in the burning heat.

Finding food

The coyote feeds on fruit and insects— whatever it can find. It also hunts for small animals.

Globemallow

Jackrabbit

Tarantula

Storing water

Like many desert plants, the organ pipe cactus can store water inside its thick, waxy stems.

Giant ears

The jackrabbit's huge ears help it listen for danger and also give off heat to help it stay cool.

Hunting at night

Rattlesnakes are expert hunters. They use heat sensors to find warm-blooded prey in the dark.

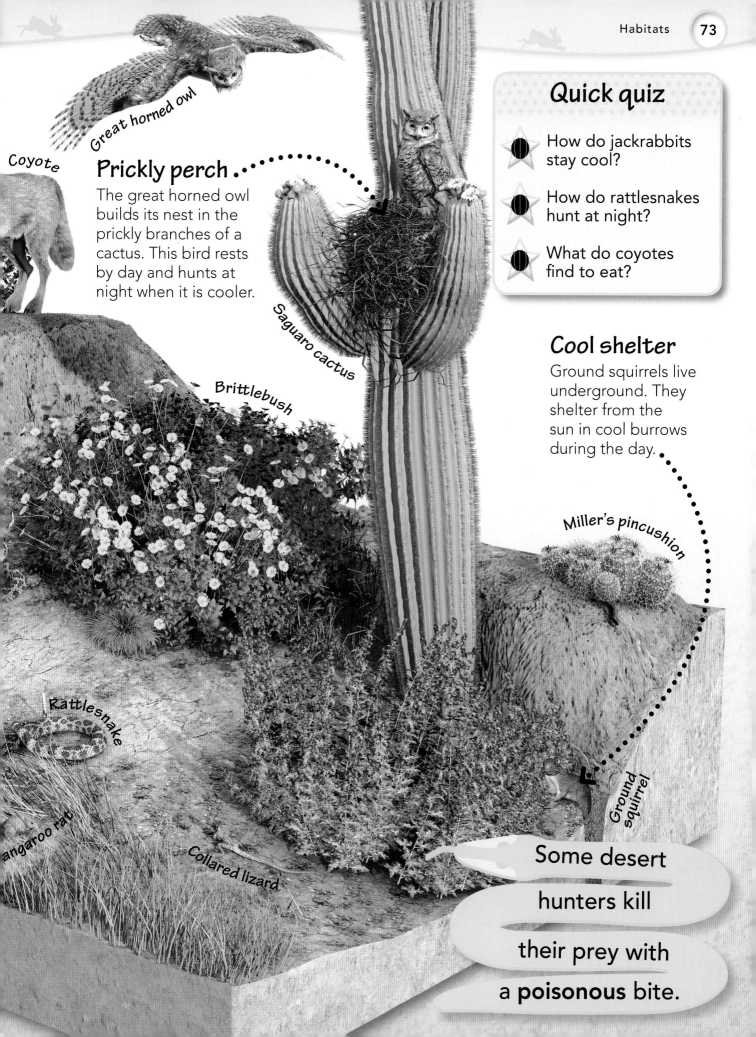

Great horned owl

Coyote

Prickly perch

The great horned owl builds its nest in the prickly branches of a cactus. This bird rests by day and hunts at night when it is cooler.

Saguaro cactus

Brittlebush

Rattlesnake

Kangaroo rat

Collared lizard

Quick quiz

★ How do jackrabbits stay cool?

★ How do rattlesnakes hunt at night?

★ What do coyotes find to eat?

Cool shelter

Ground squirrels live underground. They shelter from the sun in cool burrows during the day.

Miller's pincushion

Ground squirrel

Some desert hunters kill their prey with a **poisonous** bite.

Vulture

Umbrella trees
They may be shaped like umbrellas, but acacia trees can live for months without rain.

Leading lion
The male lion is head of his family group, which is called a pride. He lets the lioness hunt for food but is always first to eat.

Wildebeest

Cheetah

Do lions live in the jungle?

Lions don't live in the wet and steamy jungle (also known as a rain forest). They prefer the dry, open grasslands of Africa, which are called savannas. The savanna gets enough rain for shrubs and some trees to grow, and it is home to many different kinds of animal.

A **lion's roar** can be heard up to **5 miles (8 km)** away.

Eating leftovers

Vultures are large birds that are scavengers. They eat the remains of the prey left behind by other animals.

Elephant

Vulture

Gazelle

Zebra

The long trek

Many animals that live on the savanna, such as wildebeest, zebra, and gazelle, migrate at certain times of year. This means that they travel hundreds of miles seeking fresh grass for grazing.

Water danger

While zebra drink at the water hole, they look out for danger. Lions, cheetahs, and leopards will lurk nearby, hunting for prey.

Quick quiz

What is another name for a jungle?

What is a family of lions called?

Which trees look like umbrellas?

What is a rain forest?

A rain forest (also called a jungle) is a place where lots of different types of tree grow. Tropical rain forests have hot, humid, rainy weather all year round. More than half of all plant and animal species live in rain forests such as the Amazon in Brazil.

Scarlet macaw

Flying high •••••••••••••••••

Colorful scarlet macaws, a kind of parrot, fly from tree to tree to feed on nuts and fruit.

Toucan

Top to bottom

A rain forest has different layers where animals live or find food. "Emergent trees" grow up above the main canopy (tree tops). They get bright sunlight, while the forest floor doesn't get much light at all.

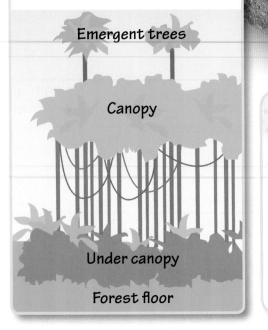

Emergent trees

Canopy

Under canopy

Forest floor

Piranha

Black caiman

Giant otter

Amazon River

Quick quiz

★ What do scarlet macaws feed on?

★ How does the emerald tree boa kill prey?

★ Do jaguars always stay on the forest floor?

Harpy eagle

Blue-and-
yellow macaw

Howler monkey

Swooping in
When a harpy eagle sees a monkey or sloth in the trees, it swoops down to grab it in its strong claws.

Monkeying around
Howler monkeys live in the canopy and feed on leaves. They wake up the rain forest at dawn with their loud howls.

Rain forests cover less than **6 percent** of the Earth's surface.

Snakes alive
An emerald tree boa blends in among the green leaves. It squeezes its prey to death.

On the prowl
A jaguar roams the forest floor looking for prey. It can also climb trees and will even swim in the river.

Emerald
tree boa

Capybara

Green
iguana

Jaguar

Giant
water lily

History

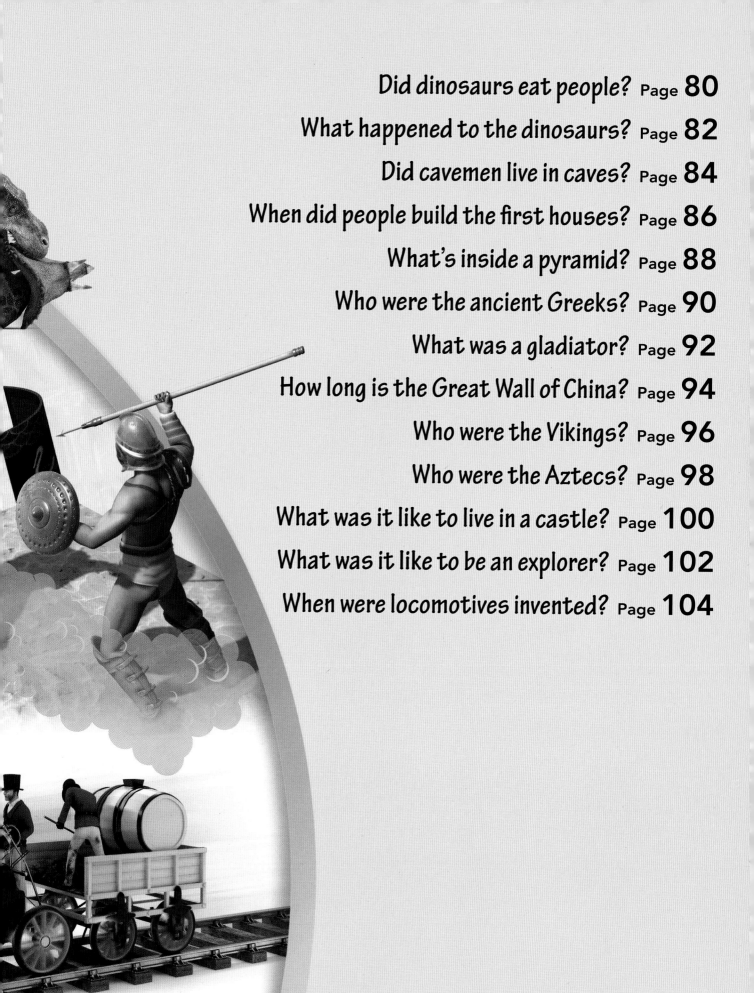

Did dinosaurs eat people?

Dinosaurs ate plants or other animals or dinosaurs, but not people! The idea of a Tyrannosaurus rex (T. rex) snacking on humans is an invention of films. Massive meat-eaters died out millions of years before humans appeared on the Earth.

Quick quiz

 How many teeth did a T. rex have?

 What did it use its tail for?

 What were pterodactyls?

Scary smiles

A T. rex had 60 teeth that were as long and sharp as knives. This helped the meat-eating dinosaur cut through the flesh of its prey.

Open wide

Meat-eating dinosaurs had massive jaws that opened extra wide.

Balancing tails

The T. rex had a long tail that it used to help it balance when running. Plant-eating dinosaurs, meanwhile, had large, heavy tails they could use to defend themselves against predators.

A T. rex was about 40 ft (12 m) long— as long as a bus!

Giant reptiles

Dinosaurs were reptiles that lived from 230 million to 66 million years ago. However, not all reptiles were dinosaurs. Pterodactyls were flying reptiles, and there were other reptiles that lived in the sea.

Short legs

The T. rex had a huge, heavy body and rather short legs. It was a fearsome predator that could run as fast as the plant-eating dinosaurs.

What happened to the dinosaurs?

Sixty-six million years ago, the dinosaurs died out. No one knows exactly what happened, but it is possible that a big asteroid hit the Earth and the dinosaurs could not survive the changes that it caused.

Quick quiz

 When did the dinosaurs die out?

 Why did meat-eating dinosaurs starve?

 How big is the asteroid crater?

Starving dinosaurs
Plant-eating dinosaurs had no plants to eat, so they starved to death. This meant that the meat-eaters eventually had no food either, and starved to death, too.

Some animals still survive from this time. These include **scorpions, turtles, crocodiles, birds,** and **insects**.

Dusty sky

Huge clouds of dust were thrown up into the sky when the asteroid hit the ground. They blocked out the sunlight, which turned the planet cold and dark for many years.

Dying plants

Hot debris from the asteroid started fires that destroyed plants. They could not grow again because the dust in the sky blocked out the sunlight they needed to survive.

Making an impact

It is thought that the asteroid that hit the Earth was 6 miles (10 km) across! The crater caused by the impact is 110 miles (180 km) wide. It was discovered in 1990, in a town called Chicxulub, in Mexico.

Did cavemen live in caves?

Tens of thousands of years ago, some early people used caves to shelter from the weather or to hide from wild animals. It's thought they mostly used caves for short periods, however, and did not settle in them.

Early people often used

Cave painting

We know about early people because the cave paintings they made showed important events in their lives. This painting was probably made by Cro-Magnon people in around 15,000 BCE.

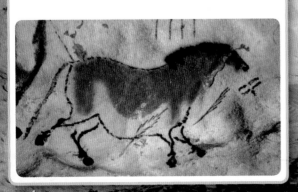

Room for one more

Most caves were only big enough for small groups. It's thought that Neanderthal people lived in groups of around 12 people.

caves while out hunting for food.

Early people

When people talk about cavemen, they often mean Neanderthals. This early form of human had a heavy build, which helped protect against cold weather. They died out around 30,000 years ago.

Quick quiz

- Why did early people shelter in caves?

- How many people lived in one cave?

- When did the Neanderthals die out?

Several **different species of early humans** used caves for shelter.

When did people build the first houses?

Early humans were hunters who moved around to find food, so they lived in temporary shelters. Around 12,000 years ago, when people learned how to farm, they settled in one place and started to build permanent houses. Over time, these groups of houses became towns like this one, which existed 9,000 years ago.

Drying out
Animal skins were cleaned and dried and used for clothing.

Animal skin

Rooftop life
People used roofs as spaces to do their work. There were no streets in the cramped town, so that it would be hard for attackers to enter.

Roof made of reeds

Ox

Quick quiz

 How old is the town shown here?

 What did farm animals provide?

 Why did people weave cloth?

Farm animals
Cattle, sheep, donkeys, and goats were kept in pens between the houses. They provided people with food, wool, and transportation.

Cloth shelter

Colorful cloth
Early people were
skilled at weaving cloth
for clothes, blankets,
and decoration.

Houses had
no front doors!
Instead, people
used **hatches in
the roofs.**

Entrance hatch

Ox

Wall
painting

Goats

Sheep

Interior design
Some houses were
decorated with wall
paintings, which showed
scenes from everyday life.

Under the floor
In this town, people who
died were buried under
the floors of houses.

What's inside a pyramid?

The Great Pyramid of Giza, on the banks of the Nile River in Egypt, was built as a tomb to contain the body of Egypt's ruler, the pharaoh Khufu. The huge pyramid is built from more than two million stone blocks stacked into 200 layers.

The Great Pyramid was built 4,500 years ago.

1 Fit for a king
Deep inside the pyramid, at the end of a long passage, is the King's Chamber. This room once contained Khufu's mummified remains.

2 On the outside
Today, the outside of the Great Pyramid is stepped. When it was first built, the stones were covered with a layer of polished limestone.

It took more than 20 years to build the Great Pyramid.

Hieroglyphics

The Ancient Egyptians had a civilization that lasted more than 3,000 years. They left behind lots of clues about their lives, including texts written in hieroglyphs, which are small pictures.

3 In the middle

The Middle Chamber was originally called the Queen's Chamber. It is thought to have contained a statue of the king as well as items such as furniture, tools, and weapons.

4 A long walk

The Grand Gallery leads to the King's Chamber. It is nearly 165 ft (50 m) long. In one section its ceiling is an incredible 26 ft (8 m) high.

5 This way in

Today's entrance was created in the year 820 CE. It was made by robbers when they were breaking into the pyramid.

Quick quiz

 Where is the Great Pyramid of Giza?

 What was inside the King's Chamber?

 What is the Queen's Chamber now called?

Who were the ancient Greeks?

The ancient Greeks were famous thinkers. Some of their ideas in science, art, and politics are still used today. They worshiped many gods and goddesses and built temples dedicated to them. This one is the Parthenon in Athens. It was built to honor the goddess Athena.

The **Parthenon** was built around **2,500 years ago** and still stands today.

Story statues ....

The sculptures above the entrance tell the story of Athena's birth. She was goddess of wisdom and courage in battle.

Quick quiz

 Where is the Parthenon?

 What was the statue of Athena covered in?

 When were the first Olympic Games?

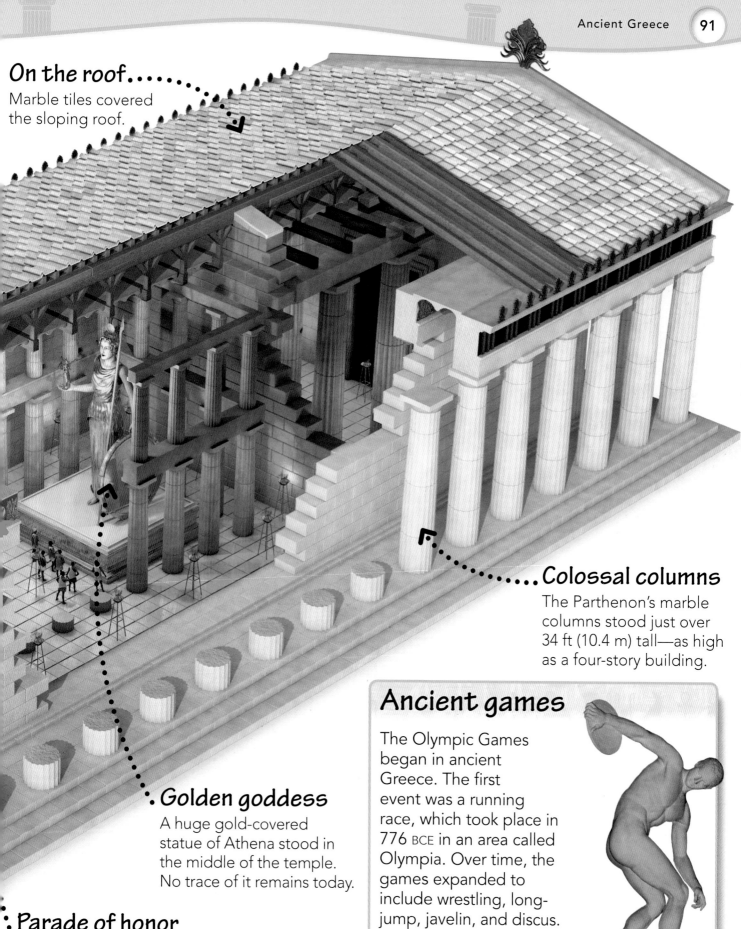

On the roof......
Marble tiles covered the sloping roof.

Colossal columns
The Parthenon's marble columns stood just over 34 ft (10.4 m) tall—as high as a four-story building.

Golden goddess
A huge gold-covered statue of Athena stood in the middle of the temple. No trace of it remains today.

Parade of honor
The decoration along the inner wall, behind the pillars, shows people worshiping Athena.

Ancient games
The Olympic Games began in ancient Greece. The first event was a running race, which took place in 776 BCE in an area called Olympia. Over time, the games expanded to include wrestling, long-jump, javelin, and discus.

Statue of a discus thrower

What was a gladiator?

Two thousand years ago, in Roman cities, crowds gathered to be entertained by watching people fight. The fighters were called gladiators, and sometimes they fought to the death. There were more than 20 types of gladiator, who fought with different weapons.

Short sword

Some gladiators fought with a short, curved sword called a sica.

Animals, too!

Before the gladiators stepped into the arena, the crowds were entertained by trained hunters who would fight animals such as lions and wolves.

The **first gladiators** were **prisoners** from countries invaded by the Roman army.

Protecting the body...

A gladiator's shield was large and oblong, or small and round, depending on the weapon he carried.

... and the head

Headgear was made to be showy to impress people, as well as to provide good protection.

Sharp spear

Some gladiators used long spears to jab at their opponents. The spears were wooden poles tipped with an iron point.

Quick quiz

 How many types of gladiator were there?

 Was a sica a spear or a sword?

 What did gladiators wear on their feet?

Gladiators fought on sand.

·· Mix and match

Gladiators often wore protective leg armor, but not everyone had the same armor or weapons. The crowds enjoyed seeing how the differences affected the fights.

No shoes!

Gladiators fought in bare feet or wore leather sandals with straps.

How long is the Great Wall of China?

Around 1,080 miles (1,740 km) of the Great Wall stands today, but no one really knows how far it stretched at its longest, 500 years ago. Estimates range from 5,500 miles (8,850 km) to more than 13,000 miles (21,000 km) in total.

Wide walls
The widest parts of the wall were 30 ft (9 m) across. At its narrowest, the wall was just 12 in (30 cm) wide—the length of a ruler).

The top of the Great Wall was used as a road.

Signal towers
Signal towers were built along the wall. Messages, such as warnings of invasions, were sent from one tower to another.

Where the wall was

This map shows where the wall was 500 years ago. At first, there were several short walls, which were built 2,800 years ago. They were joined together about 400 years later and were added to over time.

Beijing

China

0 km   1000

0 miles   1000

The first walls were built to **stop northern tribes** from **invading** farmland.

Alarm calls
A cannon was used to send loud warning signals if enemies were going to attack.

Smoke signals
Fires burned by the towers. They were used to send smoke signals during the day, to warn of attacks or to get help.

Quick quiz

★ How much of the wall is standing today?

★ Why were smoke signals sent?

★ How many people built the wall?

On the look out
Soldiers guarded each section of the wall, looking out for invaders.

Lots of labor
It took hundreds of thousands of people to build the Great Wall.

Who were the Vikings?

The Vikings lived in Scandinavia, in northern Europe, more than 1,000 years ago. They were fierce warriors known for their attacks and raids, but they also traded and made long journeys to different parts of the world. Their warships, called longboats, had a sail to cross oceans, but could also be rowed up rivers.

Big and bright.
Longships had one large sail made from thick woolen cloth. It is thought that sails were patterned with bright stripes.

A fearsome sight
Vikings carved and attached wooden heads of fearsome creatures, such as dragons, to the front of their longships.

"Viking" comes from an old Norwegian word, vikingr, which means "sea-raider."

Viking travelers

The Vikings were the first people to live in Iceland and they sailed even farther to Greenland and North America. Many set up homes in the places they reached.

Viking warriors

Armor plating
Rowers lined up their shields along the sides of the boat for protection.

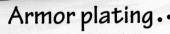

Quick quiz

Where did the Vikings live?

What was the sail made from?

How many men steered the boat?

Turn left!

An extra-long oar was used for steering. It was attached to the back of the boat and turned by one man.

All pull together

The longship had holes in each side for long oars to pass through. When the sail was up, the sailors would pull in their oars and cover the holes to keep out the water.

Who were the Aztecs?

The Aztecs were fierce warriors who built an empire in Mexico from the 1300s to the 1500s. They had a very advanced society, with markets, schools, temples, and art. Their capital was Tenochtitlán, and in its center was the Templo Mayor—a huge pyramid with two temples on top.

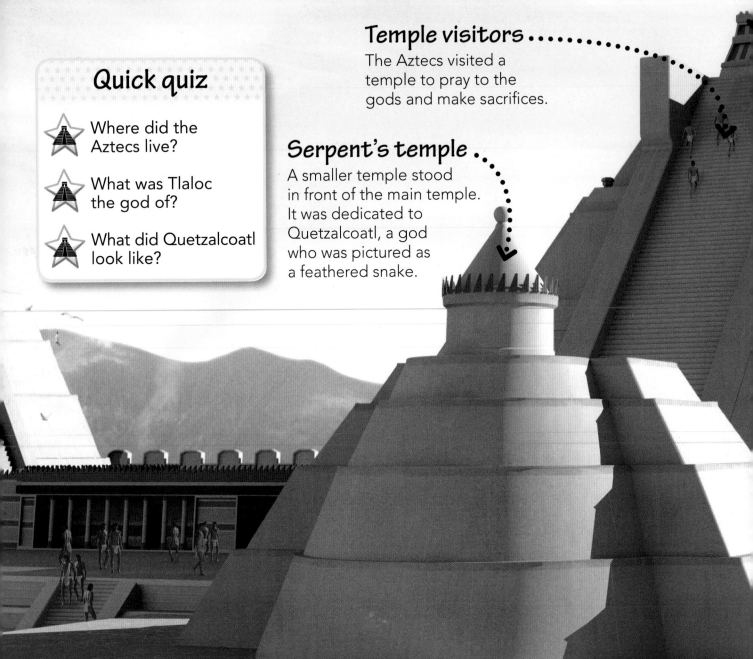

Praying for rain
This temple was dedicated to Tlaloc, the god of rain and farming.

Temple visitors
The Aztecs visited a temple to pray to the gods and make sacrifices.

Serpent's temple
A smaller temple stood in front of the main temple. It was dedicated to Quetzalcoatl, a god who was pictured as a feathered snake.

Quick quiz

★ Where did the Aztecs live?

★ What was Tlaloc the god of?

★ What did Quetzalcoatl look like?

The Templo Mayor was rebuilt **seven times**, but finally **destroyed** in 1521.

War god
This temple was dedicated to Huitzilopochtli, the god of war.

Ancient Americas

Three mighty civilizations ruled different parts of Central and South America from around 300 BCE until the 1500s CE. They were the Maya, the Aztecs, and the Incas.

Atlantic Ocean

Pacific Ocean

■ Aztecs
■ Maya
□ Incas

What was it like to live in a castle?

A castle could be cold, damp, dark, smelly, and drafty. After all, it was built to keep enemies out, with huge outer walls, hefty corner towers, and narrow slits instead of windows.

Look out!
Towers at the corners of the castle allowed defenders to see if enemies were coming.

Living rooms
The lord's private rooms, called the solar, were in the strongest part of the castle.

Don't cross the water
A deep moat filled with water ran around the castle. It kept attackers away from the walls.

Raise the drawbridge
At the castle entrance, a wooden drawbridge could be lowered to let guests in or raised to keep attackers out.

The way in
A castle had one main entrance, which made it easier to defend.

This is a **concentric castle** from the 13th century. It has two outer walls.

Fit for a feast

Inside the great hall, the lord would hold feasts for knights and guests.

Vegetable garden

Luxury living

The lord and his family lived and slept in the solar. He had a grand bed with a feather mattress, quilts, and fur covers—and linen curtains to keep out drafts.

Quick quiz

 What was the solar?

 What was a moat filled with?

 Where were feasts held?

Leisure time

The covered area called the tilla was a place where the ship's crew could relax and play games, such as dice.

What was it like to be an explorer?

In 1492, Christopher Columbus crossed the Atlantic Ocean in a ship like this one. It was a dangerous and difficult journey. He and his crew of around 90 men did not know whether they would run out of food and water, and there was a high risk of disease.

Columbus lost

Columbus sailed from Spain across the Atlantic Ocean looking for a route to East Asia. He made a mistake about the distance he sailed, and when he landed in the Americas, he thought he had reached China or Japan.

On deck

The deck was a large, open area where most activities took place. The sailors slept there, and each morning they gathered there to say prayers.

Eating out
The ship's cook made food for the crew using fresh fish, salted meat, cheese, and dried peas.

Columbus's first Atlantic crossing took **70 days**. A ship today can do this in **7 days**.

Quick quiz
 Where did Columbus think he had landed?

 What did Columbus's crew eat?

 What was on the afterdeck?

Food supplies
Below deck was the main storage area, with barrels of water and wine, beans, and a kind of biscuit called hardtack.

Self defense
The area called the afterdeck had two cannons, in case the ship was attacked.

When were locomotives invented?

The first steam-powered train engine was invented in 1804 by an English engineer named Richard Trevithick. It worked by burning coal to boil water into steam, which moved the train. In 1829, George Stephenson built the Rocket—a better, faster version of the steam locomotive.

Water supply

Water was stored in a barrel. When the engineer needed it, he made it flow through pipes to the boiler where it was turned to steam.

Engine supplies

A cart at the back of the train carried the coal and water the engine needed to make it go.

The Rocket's top speed was **29 mph (46 kph)**. Today's fastest train reaches **300 mph (480 kph)**!

The first public steam railroad opened in 1825.

Quick quiz

 Who invented the first steam train engine?

 What supplies did the engine need?

 How did the steam turn the wheels?

Fanning the flames .....
The smokestack allowed more air to travel through the firebox. This made the fire burn harder and the train go faster.

Full steam ahead
Steam from the boiler pushed a piston up and down, which turned the wheels.

Firing up
Burning coal in the firebox heated the water in the boiler.

Boiler

ROCKET.

Science

Why do ice pops melt?

When you take an ice pop out of the freezer, it is solid. Solid objects are made of tiny particles (pieces) that are packed tightly together and don't move much. As the ice pop warms up, it melts and turns into liquid. This happens because the heat gives the particles more energy and they spread out away from each other.

Frozen solid..............

A solid ice pop has a definite shape.

Free flowing.........

The melted ice has turned into a liquid, which does not have a definite shape. The liquid flows (moves) to fill the space it is in.

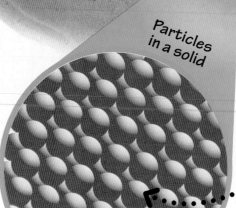

Particles in a solid

Quick quiz

 Do the particles in a frozen ice pop move?

 Does a liquid have a definite shape?

 At what temperature does water freeze?

On the spot

The particles in a solid do not have enough energy to move around. They vibrate (jiggle) slightly, but not enough for you to see.

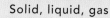

From liquid to gas

Water is a liquid, but it can be changed into a solid or a gas. When water is frozen, it turns into ice, which is a solid. When water is heated, it turns into steam, which is a gas. The particles in a gas move even faster than in a liquid and spread out in all directions.

Particles in a gas

Particles in a liquid

Breaking away

As the ice pop warms up in the air, the particles inside the ice gain more energy. This allows them to break away from each other and move around freely.

Water **freezes** into ice at **32°F** (0°C) and **boils** to become steam at **212°F** (100°C).

Why does metal get rusty?

Only iron and metals that contain iron, such as steel, get rusty. Iron rusts when it comes into contact with water and air. This is because the water and oxygen in the air react with the iron. This reaction creates a new substance—the reddish-brown flakes of rust.

Quick quiz

 What kind of metal becomes rusty?

 What are bicycle tires made of?

 Which parts of a bicycle can rust?

Rustless rubber

Bicycle tires will not rust because they are made of rubber. Rubber does not react with oxygen in the way that iron does.

Chain reaction

A bicycle chain is made of steel, so it will rust. You can prevent rust by putting oil on the chain, which helps to keep water off it.

In the saddle
A bicycle seat made of leather or plastic will not rust, but it might get torn or wear out.

Painting iron can keep it from rusting because paint helps to **keep out air and water.**

Rusty chips
A bicycle frame made of steel will become rusty if the metal is in contact with air and water for a long time. The frame is protected by paint, but if the paint is chipped, rust will form on the metal underneath.

Materials in your home

"Materials" is a word for the different stuff that things are made from, such as metal, plastic, or glass. Your home is full of objects made from different materials.

Plastic
Toy

Glass
Drinking glass

Wood
Chair

Wool
Sweater

Metal
Knife and fork

Why does fruit rot?

As soon as it is picked, fruit releases a gas called ethylene, which makes it ripen and get softer and sweeter. When the fruit gets very ripe, however, it begins to break down, or rot. At the same time, tiny, invisible molds and bacteria in the air also land on the fruit, making it ripen, and then rot, faster.

Quick quiz

 When does an apple start to rot?

 What happens to an apple's skin as it rots?

 Are all molds dangerous to eat?

Storing food in the refrigerator keeps it fresher longer.

1 Fresh fruit
The skin of a fresh, ripe apple is smooth, shiny, and colorful. The apple feels firm and tastes crisp, juicy, and sweet.

2 First wrinkles
After a week or two, the apple's skin starts to wrinkle. The color becomes dull and the apple feels softer.

3 Past its best
A few weeks later, the flesh of the apple has become mushy and soft. It still tastes sweet, but has lost some of its flavor.

Moldy meals

Not all mold is unpleasant or dangerous to eat. Adding certain molds to cheese when it is made creates "blue" cheese, which has a strong flavor and a smell that some people love.

Stilton, a blue cheese

Rotting gets rid of a fruit's flesh and **releases its seeds** so that a **new plant** can grow.

In the air

The apple turns brown when chemicals in the fruit react with oxygen in the air.

Losing water

The apple wrinkles and shrinks as water slowly evaporates from its flesh.

❹ Changing shape

After about four or five weeks, the apple starts to shrivel up. Its red skin has turned brown in places.

❺ Mold takes hold

The apple looks and smells nasty and is no longer good to eat. Mold and bacteria speed up the rotting process.

❻ Rotten fruit

After several weeks, the whole apple is rotten. It is half the size it was and is completely discolored and shriveled.

What is energy?

Energy is the ability to do work. Work can include many things, such as walking to school, turning the wheels of a car, powering a computer, or making plants and animals grow. Most of the energy on the Earth comes from the Sun.

Energy cannot be **created** or **destroyed**. It simply **changes** from one form to another.

1 Heat and light

Nuclear reactions inside the Sun change matter into light energy and heat energy. This energy travels through space to the Earth.

2 Growing plants

Plants such as wheat tak in the Sun's energy and use it to make sugars. Th wheat stores the energy from the sugars inside its cells and uses it for growth

Ready to go

When you stretch a rubber band, you use some energy. The band stores this energy for as long as you hold it. If you let it go suddenly, the rubber band then changes the stored energy into kinetic (movement) energy and sound energy, as it moves with a "boing."

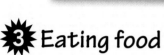

✴ 3 Eating food

Bread contains the stored energy from the wheat. When we eat it, or any other food, our bodies store the energy from the food and use it to power everything from our brains to our muscles.

Quick quiz

 Where does energy come from?

 What do plants use energy for?

 Can energy be destroyed?

✴ 4 On the move

When we run, the energy stored in our bodies changes into kinetic (movement) energy. If we kick a ball, some of this energy is passed on to the ball, making it move.

Where does electricity come from?

Most of the electricity people use in their homes comes from a power plant. The electricity travels along power lines to our homes, where we use it for cooking, heating, lighting, and running appliances like televisions.

3 On the move

The high-voltage electricity is carried along power lines supported by huge towers.

2 Step up

The electricity travels to a "step-up" substation, which increases the electricity's voltage (pressure that pushes it along). This makes it easier to move and wastes less energy.

Fossil fuels are formed underground from the remains of ancient plants and animals.

1 Power plant

At most power plants, fossil fuels such as coal, oil, or gas are burned to heat water to make steam. This steam turns a wheel called a turbine to make electricity.

Quick quiz

 Can you name three fossil fuels?

 What happens in a power plant?

Why is solar power a renewable energy source?

5 Coming home

The lower-voltage electricity is carried along another set of power lines and pylons to the power sockets in people's homes.

Electricity moves at 1 billion ft (300 million m) per second.

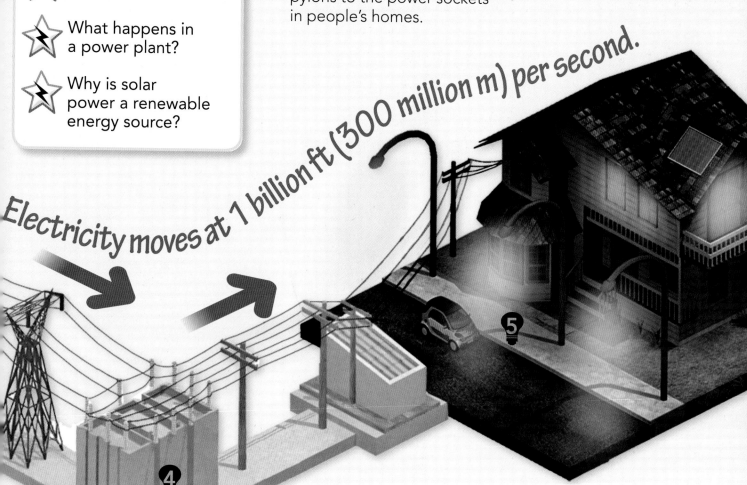

4 Step down

The electricity reaches another substation, where the electricity's voltage is reduced. This makes it safer to use in people's homes.

Energy forever

Fossil fuels are nonrenewable sources of energy: There is a fixed amount of them on the Earth and they may all be used up one day. However, there are also renewable energy sources. The power of the wind, water, or the Sun will never run out.

Hydroelectric power uses water moving through a dam to create electricity.

Wind power uses the wind to turn huge turbines, which produce electricity.

Solar power turns light from the Sun's rays into electricity.

How does a magnet work?

Magnets are usually made of a metal called iron, or metal that contains iron. Magnets attract (pull in) things made of iron, or other magnetic metals. All magnets have two ends—a north pole and a south pole.

North pole

This end of the magnet is the north pole. If it meets a north pole on another magnet, it pushes it away, but if it meets a south pole on another magnet, it attracts it (pulls toward it).

Magnetic field

Lines of magnetic force (the power that attracts magnetic metals) connect the two poles. The pattern of these lines is called the magnetic field.

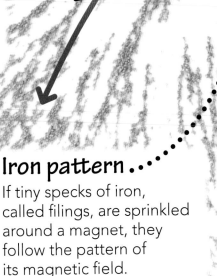

Bar magnet

Magnetic force loops

Iron pattern

If tiny specks of iron, called filings, are sprinkled around a magnet, they follow the pattern of its magnetic field.

Quick quiz

 Which metal are magnets made from?

 What are the ends of a magnet called?

 What invention uses a magnet?

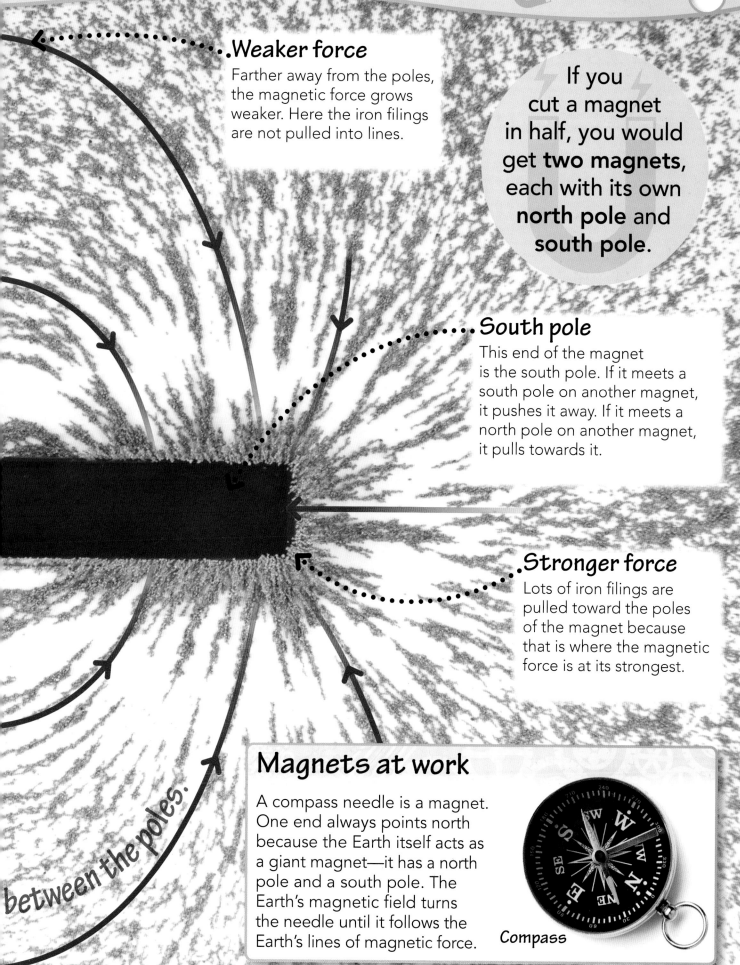

Weaker force

Farther away from the poles, the magnetic force grows weaker. Here the iron filings are not pulled into lines.

If you cut a magnet in half, you would get **two magnets**, each with its own **north pole** and **south pole**.

South pole

This end of the magnet is the south pole. If it meets a south pole on another magnet, it pushes it away. If it meets a north pole on another magnet, it pulls towards it.

Stronger force

Lots of iron filings are pulled toward the poles of the magnet because that is where the magnetic force is at its strongest.

between the poles.

Magnets at work

A compass needle is a magnet. One end always points north because the Earth itself acts as a giant magnet—it has a north pole and a south pole. The Earth's magnetic field turns the needle until it follows the Earth's lines of magnetic force.

Compass

① Sunlight

Rays of light from the Sun shine toward the falling raindrops.

When you see a rainbow, the **Sun** will always be **behind you** and the **rain** will be **in front of you**.

We see the Sun's rays as pure white light. ①

What is a rainbow?

If the Sun shines in the sky when it is raining, sunlight bounces off the raindrops and splits into different colors that you see as a rainbow. The colors you can usually see in a rainbow are red, orange, yellow, green, blue, indigo, and violet.

Quick quiz

⭐ When might you see a rainbow?

⭐ What colors are in a rainbow?

⭐ When might a red rainbow appear?

A range of rainbows

When sunlight is reflected twice in the same raindrop you may see a double rainbow—a second rainbow that sits outside the main rainbow with its colors in the opposite order. There are also lunar rainbows (when moonlight passes through raindrops) and red rainbows (which happen at dawn or dusk), but these are rare.

Double rainbow

② Splitting up

As a ray of sunlight enters a raindrop, it bends and spreads into rays going in slightly different directions. These rays now appear as different colors.

③ Bouncing back

The light bounces (reflects) off the back of the raindrop. The light shines backward and downward toward your eyes.

④ One of many

As the light leaves the raindrop, the rays spread out more. Light splitting into colors happens in every one of the millions of raindrops in the sky. Together, the drops make a multicolored rainbow.

What is an echo?

When you make a sound, invisible sound waves spread out in all directions. If the sound waves meet a hard surface like a cave ceiling or wall, they bounce back, and some sound reaches your ears. What you hear is a copy of the sound you made, only fainter.

❶ Original shout

When you shout, you make a vibration in your throat. This vibration travels away from your mouth quickly as a sound wave. A sound wave is a wave of squashed and stretched air, shown here in red.

Quick quiz

 How does sound travel through air?

 Why are echoes loud and clear in a cave?

 Which is louder, a baby or a jet engine?

❺ Hearing echoes

When the sound waves reach your ears, you hear the echoes of your shout. In a cave, echoes are clear and loud because the rocky surfaces reflect sound well.

2 Bouncing back

The sound waves reflect, or bounce, off the ceiling and walls of the cave, creating echoes.

3 Bouncing around

In a cave, there are lots of hard surfaces, all of which reflect your shout. Your shout might even bounce more than once before returning.

Decibel levels

Loudness is measured in decibels (dB). Sounds get louder as you get closer, so to compare loudnesses, you have to take distance into account. Here are some examples:

30 dB
Rustling leaves

50 dB
Quiet music

60 dB
Speaking

80 dB
Heavy traffic

115 dB
Baby crying

125 dB
Pneumatic drill

140 dB
Jet engine

4 Getting weaker

The sound waves start strong but get weaker as they spread out. By the time they reach your ears, they have become much weaker, making the echo sound much quieter.

Echoes don't take long to come back. Sound travels **1,100 ft (340 m) every second!**

What makes a car go?

Most cars are powered by an engine that uses gasoline or diesel, which are liquid fuels. The car's engine burns this fuel to move a system of rods and cogs, which turn the car's wheels and make it go.

Electric cars don't use gas, but run on **battery power** using an **electric motor.**

Reverse gear turns the wheels backward.

Quick quiz

 Which fuels power most cars?

 What does a gearbox do?

 What does a drive shaft connect to?

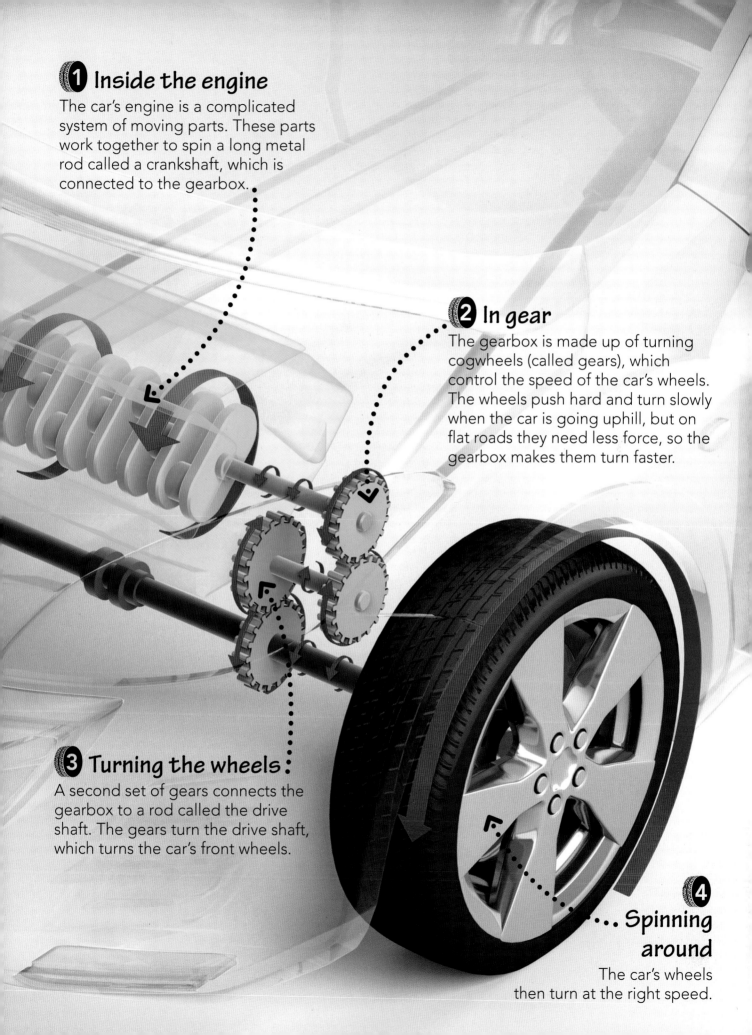

① Inside the engine

The car's engine is a complicated system of moving parts. These parts work together to spin a long metal rod called a crankshaft, which is connected to the gearbox.

② In gear

The gearbox is made up of turning cogwheels (called gears), which control the speed of the car's wheels. The wheels push hard and turn slowly when the car is going uphill, but on flat roads they need less force, so the gearbox makes them turn faster.

③ Turning the wheels

A second set of gears connects the gearbox to a rod called the drive shaft. The gears turn the drive shaft, which turns the car's front wheels.

④ ...Spinning around

The car's wheels then turn at the right speed.

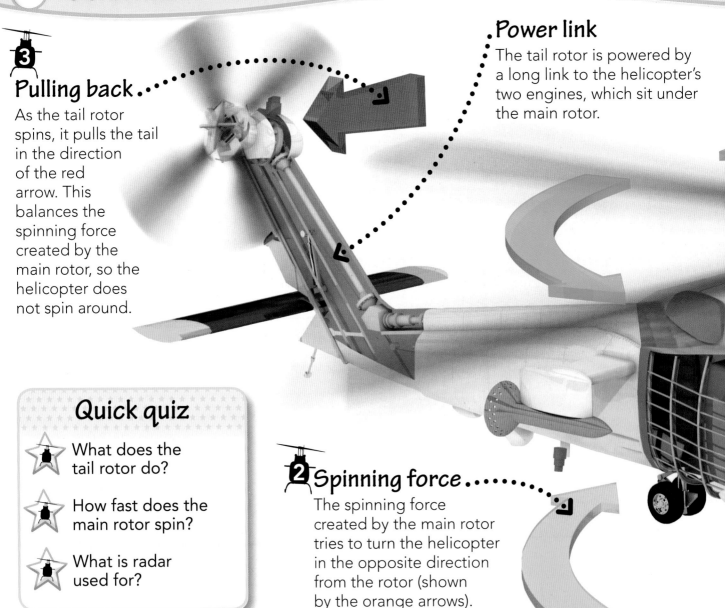

3 Pulling back

As the tail rotor spins, it pulls the tail in the direction of the red arrow. This balances the spinning force created by the main rotor, so the helicopter does not spin around.

Power link

The tail rotor is powered by a long link to the helicopter's two engines, which sit under the main rotor.

2 Spinning force

The spinning force created by the main rotor tries to turn the helicopter in the opposite direction from the rotor (shown by the orange arrows).

Quick quiz

⭐ What does the tail rotor do?

⭐ How fast does the main rotor spin?

⭐ What is radar used for?

Why does a helicopter have a propeller on its tail?

The propellers are actually called rotors, and most helicopters have two of them—the main rotor and the tail rotor. The main rotor lifts the helicopter off the ground. It also creates a spinning force that tries to spin the whole helicopter around. The tail rotor's job is to stop that from happening.

1 Spin and lift
The main rotor turns hundreds of times every minute, in the direction of the green arrows. This creates a force called lift, which raises the helicopter into the sky.

Search equipment
Radar, satellite navigation, and night-vision equipment are used to search for objects, especially at sea.

Rescue service
This search-and-rescue helicopter has a stretcher that can be lowered to pick up injured people.

Taking control
The pilot flies the helicopter by using two separate hand controls and two foot controls.

A helicopter can fly **up, down, forward, sideways, backward,** and even **hover in one place.**

Twin rotor Chinook
The Chinook helicopter has two main rotors, but no tail rotor. The main rotors turn in opposite directions. One tries to spin the helicopter one way, while the other does the opposite. They balance each other out, so no tail rotor is needed.

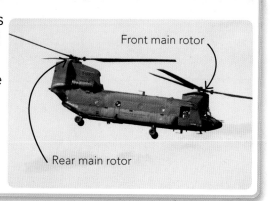
Front main rotor
Rear main rotor

How do submarines work?

A submarine does not float on the water like a boat. It travels below the surface, filling and emptying large tanks with water or air to allow it to dive and rise. The submarine shown here travels at depths of about 1,600 ft (500 m).

Propeller

In a spin
Jets of steam spin turbines in the engine room. The turbines drive a propeller at the back of the sub, which pushes it through the water.

Nuclear power
This submarine's engine is powered by nuclear energy. The energy produces heat, which makes the steam that drives the turbines.

Sleeping space
The sub's crew sleeps in cramped bunk beds. They work in shifts throughout the day and night.

Going down... and coming back up

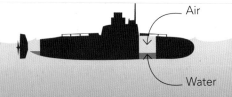

Air

Water

Staying afloat The submarine's tanks are filled with air. This allows it to float on the surface of the ocean.

Going down When the sub needs to dive down water is pumped into the tanks, replacing the air.

Rising up The sub will rise to the surface again if the water is pumped out and air is pumped in.

Quick quiz

 How does a submarine dive?

 How do submarines use sonar?

 How was the Turtle sub powered?

The first submarine

The Turtle submarine was built nearly 250 years ago. It was made of wood and had a tank at the bottom to allow it to dive and rise. The Turtle was powered by one man; he turned a handle to spin the propeller.

In control

The control room is the heart of the sub. The crew operates everything from here.

Fully armed

The submarine carries weapons. It can launch 16 missiles at once.

Submarines move faster under water than they do on the surface.

Finding its way

When a submarine is under water, it uses sound waves called sonar to find its way around and locate objects, such as enemy submarines.

Rise and dive

The sub has a tank near the front and one at the back (shown in blue). These are filled with water to make the sub dive, or air to make it rise.

How does a remote control work?

A remote control sends invisible signals called radio waves to a remote-controlled vehicle to control its movements. All remote-controlled vehicles have a transmitter to send the signals, a receiver to receive them, a motor to drive the moving parts, and a battery or other power source.

Quick quiz

 Remote contol uses what kind of waves?

 What four parts do all remote-controlled vehicles have?

 What does an antenna do?

The **first radio-controlled vehicle** was a boat, which set sail in **1898**.

Some remote-controlled vehicles are large enough to ride in.

Sending signals

The antenna on the transmitter turns electric current from the battery into radio waves, which it sends to the helicopter.

In control

The controls can be moved left, right, forward, or backward to drive the helicopter.

Invisible waves

Radio waves are invisible waves of energy. The height, width, and pattern of the waves tell the helicopter to change direction or speed.

In a spin

The helicopter's rotor blades tilt when the toy receives a signal to change its direction of flight.

Not too far!

The radio waves get weaker the farther away they are from the transmitter. If the helicopter strays too far, the transmitter will lose control of it.

Receiving signals

An antenna inside the helicopter receives the signal from the transmitter.

Remote control in space

The two Voyager spacecraft were sent into space in 1977 to take photographs of planets and moons in our solar system. Even though they are now 12 billion miles (20 billion km) away, they are still controlled from our planet. The Voyagers receive the faint radio signals using sensitive receivers pointed directly at transmitters on the Earth.

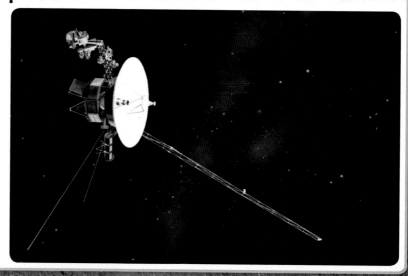

How do cell phones work?

When a person sends a text, the cell phone sends it as invisible radio waves to a tower called a base station. There are lots of base stations, which are connected by computers inside a building called a switching office. These computers pass the message on from one base station to another, and then on to the phone being called.

Radio waves

First base station

The **first text message** was sent in 1992 in the UK. It said, **"Merry Christmas."**

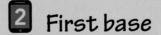

1 Press send

When a text message is sent, the phone sends the message through the air as invisible radio waves. These are picked up by the nearest base station (a special tower with an antenna on top).

2 First base

The base station receives the radio waves and sends them as an electronic signal along an underground cable to a network of computers inside a building called a switching office.

"Cell" phones

Base stations are spread out across a country. Each base station stands in its own area, which is called a cell. This is how cell phones got their name.

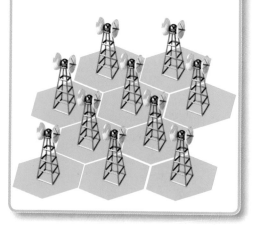

Quick quiz

 What does a phone send to a base station?

What did the first text message say?

How many base stations are in a cell?

Second base station

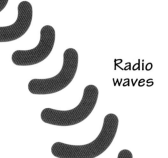

Radio waves

Switching office

HELLO

3 Switch around

The computers in the switching office find the base station nearest to the phone that the text is being sent to. It then passes the signal along cables to this base station.

4 Second base

The second base station receives the signal, turns it back into radio waves, and sends them through the air to the phone.

5 Message received!

The phone picks up the radio waves and changes them back into the original message.

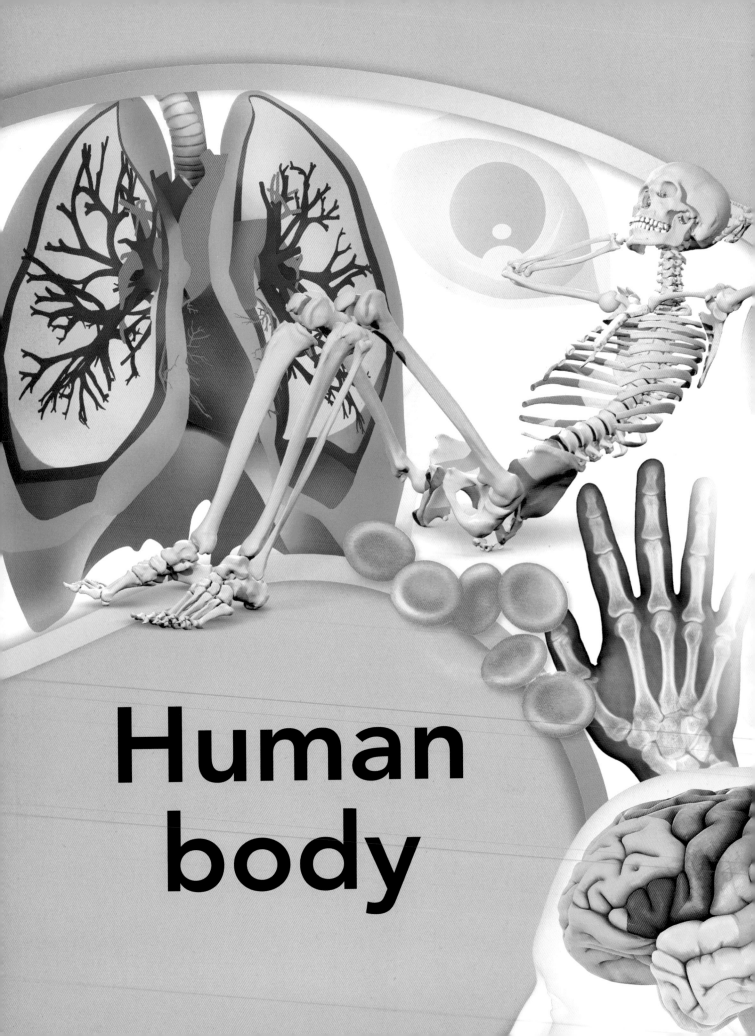

Human body

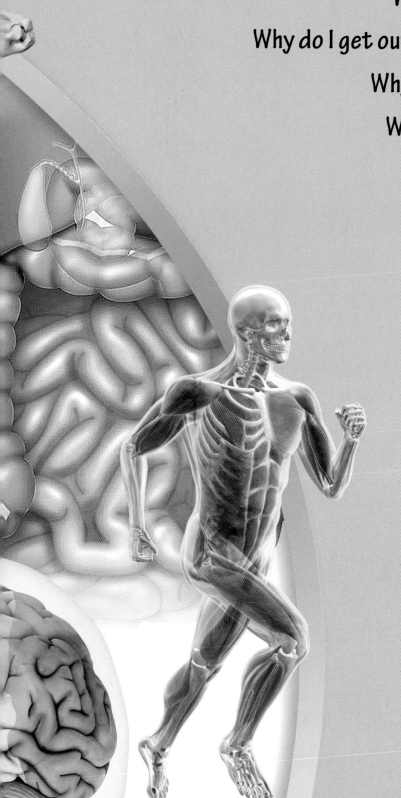

What's inside my body?

Your body is made up of trillions of tiny living things called cells. They combine to form tissues, including muscles and nerves. Groups of tissues working together make organs, such as your brain and heart.

Control center

You need your brain to move and think. Without it, the rest of your body could do nothing at all.

Wobble box

When air from your breath passes over your larynx (or voice box), the cords inside it wobble. This makes sounds, allowing you to speak.

Deep breaths

When you breathe in, your lungs take in oxygen from the air. When you breathe out, they get rid of the waste gas you don't need.

Pumping blood

Your heart is a pump that sends blood around your body in one direction. It beats day and night without stopping.

Quick quiz

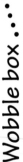 Which body part produces sound?

What is your heart used for?

Where in your body is your urine stored?

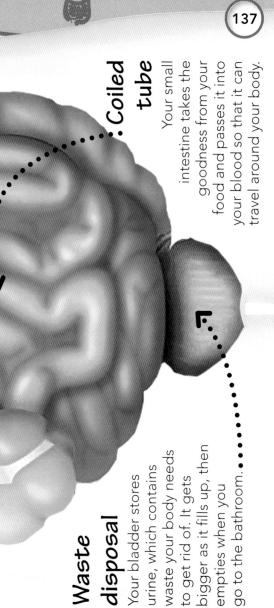

Coiled tube

Your small intestine takes the goodness from your food and passes it into your blood so that it can travel around your body.

Food processor

Your liver is like a mini factory. It takes the food you eat, separates the good parts from the bad, then sends them to the right parts of your body.

We have about the same number of **hairs** on our body as **a chimpanzee.**

Food collector

Your stomach is a bag made of muscle. The stomach lining makes chemicals that break down your food, so your body gets the nutrients it needs.

Waste disposal

Your bladder stores urine, which contains waste your body needs to get rid of. It gets bigger as it fills up, then empties when you go to the bathroom.

A look at cells

Cells are microscopic, but without them you would not even exist. There are many different types of cell that make up parts of your body, such as blood, bones, muscles, and fat.

A fat cell shown 250 times its size and colored purple.

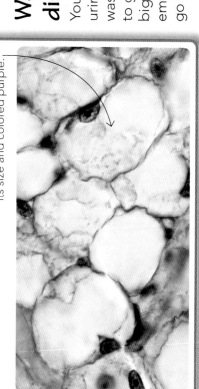

Why do I get hungry?

You need to eat food to give you energy for playing, thinking, and growing—and everything else you do. When your stomach is empty, a chemical inside it sends a message to your brain telling you that it's time to eat.

Pulpy mash

You use your teeth and tongue to mash food into a pulp. Your tongue then pushes the pulp to the back of your throat, so you can swallow it.

Slimy saliva

Your salivary glands (shown in yellow) produce saliva (or spit). Saliva makes food wetter, which helps you to swallow it.

Your stomach can **stretch to 20 times** its size after you eat.

Churning food

Strong muscles in your stomach churn your food into a creamy liquid. This makes it easier to digest (absorb the goodness).

Down the tube

After you swallow food, it travels down a tube called the esophagus. After about 10 seconds, it reaches your stomach.

Food factory

Your liver is a kind of food factory, performing lots of jobs. It makes sure the different parts of your food go to the right places in your body.

Quick quiz

 How do you know when you need to eat?

 Where does most digestion take place?

 Where is your feces made?

Juice maker
Your pancreas makes digestive juices—strong chemicals that help to break down the food.

Journey's end
Your feces travels through a tube called the rectum, then out of your body.

Waste
Your large intestine absorbs water from the food, leaving behind the waste food you don't need. This is called feces.

Breaking down fat
Your gall bladder stores bile, a chemical that helps to break down the fat in food into tiny droplets.

All the goodness
Your small intestine is where most of the digestion takes place. The food is broken down so nutrients (goodness) can be taken out of it and sent around your body.

Inside the stomach
Your stomach is a bag made of muscle. It stores your food and also starts to digest it.

During a meal, your stomach fills with food and digestive juices. The walls of your stomach squeeze to churn it all up and break down the food.

Around four hours later, the food has turned to liquid. A gap at the bottom of your stomach opens and releases the liquid into your small intestine a little at a time.

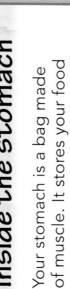

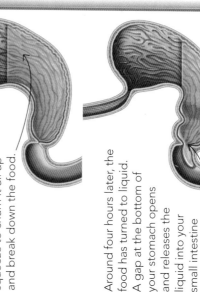

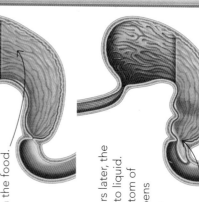

How many bones are in my body?

The human body contains 206 bones. More than half of these are in your hands and feet. Bones make up a frame for your body, called a skeleton. They also work with your muscles to help you move and protect your organs.

Hinged at the knees

The place where two bones meet is called a joint. The knee is the largest joint in your body and bends like a hinge.

One-sixth of your body weight is bone.

Thighbone (femur)

Shinbone (tibia)

Hip bone (pelvis)

Flexible foot

There are 26 bones in each foot. This helps to make them flexible enough for walking, jumping, and running.

Quick quiz

 What is the largest joint in your body?

 Is the skull one bone or many bones?

 How many bones make up the spine?

Super skull
The skull is made up of 22 bones, although most of these are locked together. In fact, only the lower jaw can move.

Arm bone (radius)

Elbow joint
The elbow is a hinge joint, like the knee. It lets you bend and straighten your arm.

Collarbone (clavicle)

Protective cage
Your ribs form a cage that protects the soft, delicate organs inside your body, such as your heart and lungs.

Bendy backbone
The backbone, or spine, is made up of 24 bones called vertebrae. These help you to twist and bend.

Bone is **six times stronger** than a steel bar of the same weight.

Growing bones
A baby's skeleton is mostly cartilage—the same stuff that makes up your ears. Unlike your ears, however, this cartilage stiffens into bone as a child grows.

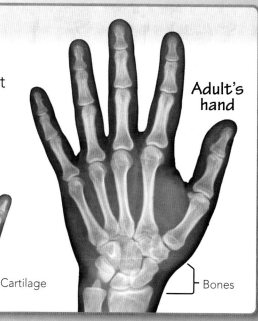

Adult's hand

Infant's hand

Cartilage

Bones

Biggest bone
The thighbone is the strongest and heaviest bone in your body. It is also the longest—a quarter of your height.

At the elbow

The movement of your elbow (the joint where your arm bones meet) is controlled by a pair of muscles called the biceps and triceps.

Quick quiz

 Where are your biceps and triceps?

 What is your biggest muscle called?

 How many muscles are in your body?

① Bending

When your biceps muscle contracts (gets shorter and thicker), it bends your elbow and pulls your lower arm toward your shoulder.

Biceps

Triceps

Why do I have muscles?

Muscles are important because they help your body to move. Without them you would not be able to walk, jump, blink, or breathe. Muscles are made of bundles of fibers, each one as thin as a hair.

Your **biggest muscle** is in your bottom. It is called the **gluteus maximus.**

Tough tendons

Your muscles are attached to your bones by tendons. They look like thin cords and are very strong.

❷ Straightening

When your triceps muscle contracts (gets shorter and thicker), it pulls your lower arm away from your shoulder.

Triceps

Pull-not-push pairs

Your body has more than 640 muscles that help you move. Like your biceps and triceps, these muscles can pull but cannot push, so they work in pairs that pull in opposite directions. For example, to move your foot, a muscle in your shin pulls it up, while a muscle at the back of your calf pulls it back down again.

Muscle pulls foot down

Muscle pulls foot up

Why do I get out of breath when I run?

When you breathe, your lungs take in air, which contains oxygen. The oxygen passes into your blood and gets carried around your body, giving you energy. When you run, your muscles need more oxygen. This makes you breathe faster and more deeply, making you feel out of breath.

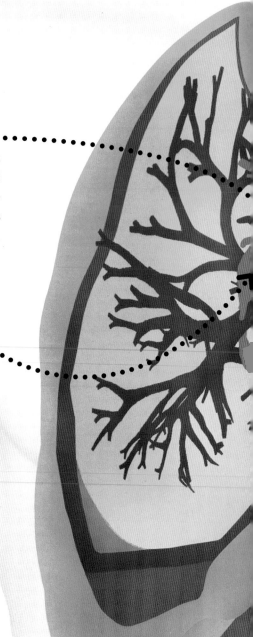

Breathe in
You suck air into your body through your nose and mouth.

Blood in
Large blood vessels (tubes that carry blood) called pulmonary arteries take blood into your lungs to pick up oxygen.

Blood out
Blood vessels called the pulmonary veins carry blood out of your lungs so that it can travel around your body.

Quick quiz

 Which arteries carry blood into your lungs?

 Are both your lungs the same size?

 What does your diaphragm do?

Your **left lung** is slightly **smaller** than your right lung, to make room for your **heart**.

Ringed tube

Your windpipe is
an airway made of
lots of rubbery rings.
These rings hold your
windpipe open so that
air can travel down it
into your lungs.

Bigger lungs, smaller lungs

When you breathe in, your lungs get bigger and
your diaphragm pulls down to give them more room.
When you breathe out, your diaphragm springs
back upward, squeezing the air out of your lungs.

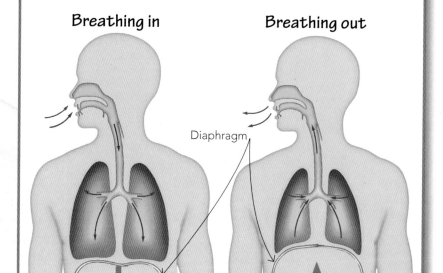

Breathing in   **Breathing out**

Diaphragm

Tubes and sacs

Your lungs are filled with thousands
of small tubes that have tiny sacs
(like bubbles) at their ends. Oxygen
travels along the tubes and through
the walls of the sacs into your blood.

At the heart

Your heart is a powerful
muscle that pumps your
blood around your body.

Muscling in

Your diaphragm is a sheet of
muscle that sits underneath
your lungs and helps you
to breathe.

Why does my heart beat?

Your heart beats to pump blood around your body through tubes called arteries and veins. Blood carries oxygen and nutrients (the goodness your body takes from your food) to give you energy.

Quick quiz

 What is your blood for?

 What is the name of your largest artery?

 What do white blood cells do?

Going to your head

One-fifth of the blood in your body is pumped to your brain.

Largest artery

The aorta is the largest artery in your body. It is about as wide as your thumb.

Muscle power

Your heart is a powerful muscle that pumps blood without taking a rest. It beats around 100,000 times per day.

From the heart

Your arteries (shown in red) carry blood that contains oxygen from your heart to the cells around your body.

Return trip

When your body has used up all of the oxygen, your veins (shown in blue) carry your blood back to your heart to get more.

Longest vein

The longest vein in your body runs from your foot to the top of your thigh. It is called the saphenous vein.

Getting smaller

Tiny tubes called capillaries transfer the blood from your arteries to your veins. They are thinner than a strand of your hair.

On average, a human heart beats at 70–80 times per minute.

Blood cells

Blood contains three types of blood cell: red blood cells for carrying oxygen around your body, white blood cells to protect you from disease, and platelet cells to help your body heal if it is injured.

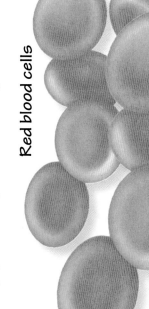

Red blood cells

What does my brain do?

You need your brain in order to think, move, see, hear, and speak. You use it to understand the world around you, and it allows you to feel emotions, such as love, anger, and excitement. Without your brain, you would not be able to do anything at all.

Your brain is covered with deep grooves and wrinkles.

Who you are
The front part of your brain controls how you think and behave.

What you say
You use this section of your brain when you speak.

What you hear
Your ears send signals to this part of your brain, so that you can hear.

Your brain uses about **one-fifth** of your **body's energy.**

Quick quiz

Where is the thinking part of your brain?

Which area controls breathing?

What are your brain's nerve cells called?

How you move

This part of your brain tells your muscles to work.

What you feel

You use this area of your brain when you touch something.

Understanding words

When someone speaks to you, this part of your brain figures out what the words mean.

What you see

Your eyes send messages to this part of your brain, so you know what you are seeing.

How you breathe

Your brain stem controls your breathing and how fast your heart beats.

Nerve cells

The brain is made up of billions of nerve cells, called neurons. They send signals to each other, like electricity traveling through wires.

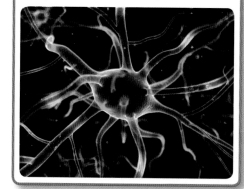

How do my eyes work?

When you look at an object, light bounces off it and enters your eye. The eye turns this into a signal that it sends to your brain. Your brain then tells you what you are seeing.

Eye color

The colored disk at the front of your eyeball is called the iris. It controls how much light gets in.

Light rays

When you look at an object, light rays bounce off that object and enter your eye.

Black hole

In the center of your iris is a tiny hole called the pupil, which looks black. The pupil lets light into your eye. It gets bigger in the dark to help you see more.

It is impossible to **sneeze** with your **eyes open.**

Into focus

The transparent lens changes shape so you can see things that are near and far away.

Just jelly!

Your eye is a squishy ball filled with a jellylike liquid. This liquid helps it to keep its round shape.

Light detection

The retina is a layer of light-sensitive cells at the back of your eye. When light hits the cells, they send messages to your brain.

Topsy turvy

The lens bends the light so everything we see is upside down. Our brain turns it the right way around again.

Roll your eyes

Six muscles move your eyeball, so you can look from side to side and up and down.

Your five senses

Humans have five senses: sight, hearing, smell, touch, and taste. Senses work together to help you understand the world.

See

Hear

Smell

Touch

Taste

To the brain

Your optic nerve carries light signals to your brain.

Quick quiz

 What is the colored part of your eye called?

 Where is your pupil?

 How do light signals reach your brain?

Why am I ticklish?

You feel ticklish because your skin is full of tiny touch sensors. When something touches you, these touch sensors send signals along nerves to your brain. A tickle can feel nice, but if it is too hard, it can become painful and your brain will send a message to your body to move away.

To the brain

The nervous system

There are billions of nerves in your body, all of which are joined together. They connect to your spinal cord (a bundle of nerves in your spine), which then connects to your brain. Nerves carry information to and from your brain at lightning speed, telling your body what to do.

Brain

Spinal cord

Nerve

Skin sensors

Billions of sensors in your skin help your brain to decide if things you touch feel cold or hot, smooth or sharp, pleasant or dangerous.

A **pain signal** travels from **your toe to your brain** in a fraction of a second.

From foot to brain

Nerves in your foot pass their signals up your leg to your spine and then to your brain. The longest nerve is your sciatic nerve. It runs from your foot all the way up your leg to your spine.

Muscle messages

Nerves also carry signals back from your spinal cord and your brain to your muscles, telling them to move.

Being tickled

When a feather tickles your feet, your touch sensors fire off lots of little signals to your brain. The brain reacts by making you laugh. This doesn't happen if you try to tickle yourself, because your brain knows how it will feel and stops its response.

Quick quiz

 What is your spinal cord?

 How many sensors are in your skin?

 What is the longest nerve in your body?

Why *do* I sneeze?

Sneezing helps your body to get rid of something it doesn't want inside it. If you breathe in tiny grains of dust or plant pollen, they tickle the inside of your nose, making you sneeze them out. Cold germs also make you sneeze, but sneezing out the germs can pass them on to other people.

Dirt catchers

Tiny hairs in your nose help catch grains of dirt that you breathe in, so they do not enter your lungs.

Speedy sneezing

When you sneeze, the mucus droplets fly out at speeds of up to 25 mph (40 kph). That's as fast as sprinter Usain Bolt can run!

Washing hands

If you sneeze out the cold virus, it can live for hours on many objects that people touch, such as door handles, phones, and skin. Washing your hands helps to get rid of the virus and keep you healthy.

The world's longest ever sneezing fit lasted **978 days!**

Sneezing uses muscles in your belly, chest, nose, and throat.

Quick quiz

 Name two things that make you sneeze.

 What are the hairs in your nose for?

 What does mucus contain?

Ha-choo!
The droplets you sneeze out are called mucus. If you have a cold and other people breathe in your mucus, they can catch your cold.

Pollen grain

Pollen grain

Bacteria

Pollen grain

Dust

Cold virus

Dust

Inside the droplets...
Each droplet can contain many different things, including living things. This picture magnifies them thousands of times.

Index

Use these pages to help you find what you're looking for in the book.

Acknowledgments

Reviewers for the Smithsonian National Museum of Natural History: Dr. Don E. Wilson, Curator Emeritus, Department of Vertebrate Zoology; Sally Kuhn Sennert, USGS/Global Volcanism Program, Department of Mineral Sciences; Dr. Michael Brett-Surman, Museum Specialist for Fossil Dinosaurs, Reptiles, Amphibians, and Fish, Department of Paleobiology; Salima Ikram, Egyptology Unit Head, Department of Anthropology; Dr. William W. Fitzhugh, Curator of Archaeology and Director of Arctic Studies Center, Department of Anthropology; J. Daniel Rogers, Curator of Archaeology, Department of Anthropology; Laetitia Plaisance, Marine Biology, Department of Invertebrate Zoology; Jeremy F. Jacobs, Collections Manager, Division of Amphibians and Reptiles.

National Air and Space Museum: Dr. F. Robert van der Linden, Chairman, Aeronautics Division; Roger Connor, Curator, Aeronautics Division; Andrew Johnston, Geographer, Center for Earth and Planetary Studies.

Freer Gallery of Art and Arthur M. Sackler Gallery: Dr. Alexander Nagel, Assistant Curator of Ancient Near East; James T. Ulak, Senior Curator of Japanese Art; Keith Wilson, Curator of Ancient Chinese Art.

National Museum of American History: L. Susan Tolbert, Deputy Chair and Curator, Division of Work and Industry; Roger E. Sherman, Associate Curator, Division of Medicine and Science.

National Zoological Park: Sara Hallager, Curator, Bird House; Lori Smith, Animal Keeper; Debra Talbott, Animal Keeper; Brian Gratwicke, Interdisciplinary Research Biologist, Smithsonian Conservation Biology Institute; Alan Peters, Curator, Invertebrates; Michael Miller, Animal Keeper, Invertebrates; Donna Stockton, Biologist, Invertebrate Exhibit; Jennifer Zoon, Communications Assistant.

Dorling Kindersley would like to thank: Bharti Bedi, Simon Holland, and Simon Mumford for editorial help.

The publisher would like to thank the following for their kind permission to reproduce their photographs:

(Key: a-above; b-below/bottom; c-center; f-far; l-left; r-right; t-top)

1 Fotolia: DM7 (bc); Primal Pictures Ltd: (crb). **4 NASA:** JPL-Caltech (tr). **4-5 Science Photo Library:** Henning Dalhoff (c). **6 ESO:** http://creativecommons.org/licenses/by/3.0 (bl). **NASA and The Hubble Heritage Team (AURA/STScI):** ESA / A. Aloisi (bl/Irregular); ESA (clb/separate exposures, clb). **8 Dorling Kindersley:** NASA (clb). **Dreamstime.com:** Bradcollett (bc). **10 Dreamstime.com:** Rosinka (l). **10-11 Pascal Henry,www.lesud.com:** (bl). **12 NASA:** (bc). **13 Dreamstime.com:** Yael Weiss (cr/Magnifying glass). **NASA:** JPL / University of Colorado (cr). **14 NASA:** Neil Armstrong, Apollo 11 Crew / GRIN (bl). **16-17 Science Photo Library:** Henning Dalhoff (c). **16 Dreamstime.com:** Pytyczech (bc). **19 NASA:** Max Planck Institute for Solar System Research (cr). **20 Dreamstime.com:** Luca Oleastri (bl). **20-21 NASA:** (b). **21 Dreamstime.com:** Themoderncanvas (cl). **22-23 NASA:** JPL-Caltech. **25 Dreamstime.com:** Yulia87 (clb). **26-27 Dreamstime.com:** Roberto Giovannini (t). **30 Corbis:** Reuters (bl). **33 Corbis:** Tui De Roy / Minden Pictures (tc). **35 Corbis:** Ralph White (cr). **36-37 Dreamstime.com:** Yulia87 (Background). **38-39 Corbis. 39 Science Photo Library:** Frank Zullo (cr). **40-41 Corbis:** Eric Nguyen. **40 Corbis:** Meijert de Haan / epa (bl). **42 Dreamstime.com:** Rosinka (l). **43 Dreamstime.com:** Kenneth Keifer | (br). **44 Dorling Kindersley:** Peter Minister, Digital Sculptor / Andrew Kerr (cl). **Dreamstime.com:** Skypixel (cb). **45 Dreamstime.com:** Stefan Hermans (bc). **46 Dreamstime.com:** Yael Weiss (br). **46-47 Dreamstime.com:** Roberto Giovannini (t). **48-49 Getty Images:** Gary Vestal / Photographer's Choice (c). **50 Alamy Images:** Simon Belcher (bl). **54-55 Corbis:** Alissa Crandall (c). **55 Dreamstime.com:** Hotshotsworldwide (tc). **Fotolia:** Mark Higgins (tr). **59 Corbis:** Rod Patterson / Gallo Images (br). **61 Dorling Kindersley:** Twan Leenders (tr). **62-63 Dreamstime.com:** Stefan Hermans (c). **63 Getty Images:** Auscape / UIG (br). **64-65 Dorling Kindersley:** Peter Minister, Digital Sculptor / Andrew Kerr (c). **65 Dreamstime.com:** Siloto (crb). **66-67 Dreamstime.com:** Haramambura (Background). **67 Alamy Images:** Alfred Schauhuber / Imagebroker (tc/blue bottle fly). **Getty Images:** Stephen Dalton / Minden Pictures (tc). **68 Dreamstime.com:** Musat Christian (bl). **68-69 Dorling Kindersley:** Andrew Kerr (c). **75 Alamy Images:** Ariadne Van Zandbergen (cr). **80-81 Dorling Kindersley:** Peter Minister, Digital Sculptor / Arran Lewis (c). **81 Dorling Kindersley:** Andrew Kerr

(br). **82-83 Dorling Kindersley:** Bedrock Studios (b). Photoshot: Daniel Heuclin / NHPA (Background). **83 Science Photo Library:** John Foster (br). **84-85 Alamy Images:** Aurora Photos. **84 Corbis:** Robert Harding World Imagery (cl). **Dorling Kindersley:** Natural History Museum, London (br/Prehistoric flint); Pitt Rivers Museum, University of Oxford (br); The Science Museum, London (br/Stone Age stone). **89 Dreamstime.com:** Diego Elorza (cra). **96-97 Dreamstime.com:** Seamartini (b). **99 Dreamstime.com:** Dariusz Kopestynski (br). **102-103 Dreamstime.com:** Seamartini (b). **102 Alamy Images:** Niday Picture Library (bc). **106-107 Dreamstime.com:** Pakwat69 (bc). **106 Corbis:** Martin Gallagher (cl). **109 Dreamstime.com:** Lightpoet (cr). **110-111 Getty Images:** Johanna Parkin / Stone. **111 Dreamstime.com:** Cloki (crb); Juan Moyano (bc). **112-113 Corbis:** Martin Gallagher (b). **Dreamstime.com:** Haramambura (Background). **114 Dreamstime.com:** Rosinka (l). **114-115 Dreamstime.com:** Roberto Giovannini (Background). **115 Pearson Asset Library:** Coleman Yuen (tc). **117 Dreamstime.com:** Rafael Angel Irusta Machin (br); Stanislav Tiplyashin (bl); Yegor Sachko (bc). **120 Dreamstime.com:** James Wheeler (br). **123 Dreamstime.com:** Marbury67 (crb). **124-125 Dreamstime.com:** Jason Winter. **127 Dreamstime.com:** Peter Zijlstra (bc). **129 Getty Images:** Science & Society Picture Library (tr). **130-131 Dreamstime.com:** Jorge Salcedo (b). **130 Dreamstime.com:** Pakwat69 (b). **131 Dreamstime.com:** Nevodka (c). **NASA:** JPL (b). **132 Dreamstime.com:** Blotty (r); Tuulijumala (bc). **132-133 Dreamstime.com:** Roberto Giovannini (t); Lbarn (bc). **133 Dreamstime.com:** Blotty (c); Tuulijumala (br). **134 Primal Pictures Ltd:** (tr); **Fotolia:** Natallia Yaumenenka / eAlisa (crb). **137 Getty Images:** Ed Reschke / Photolibrary (br). **140-141 Primal Pictures Ltd:** (c). **141 Fotolia:** Natallia Yaumenenka / eAlisa (br). **Science Photo Library:** Aj Photo (bc). **142-143 Getty Images:** MedicalRF.com (t). **143 Dreamstime.com:** Rayuken (tc). **149 Corbis:** Sebastian Kaulitzki / Science Photo Library (br). **151 Corbis:** Sean De Burca (cra). **152-153 Dreamstime.com:** Rick Sargeant (t). **154 PunchStock:** Stockbyte (bl). **154-155 Dreamstime.com:** Sebastian Kaulitzki (br)

All other images © Dorling Kindersley
For further information see: www.dkimages.com